Right on White Time

I0423450

The Black Spring Manual for Reparations Recover Agents with Justin W. R. Justice and T. Spoone Slickens

Black Power Heroes

Black Spring is dedicated to the army of innocent, unarmed, Black Power Youth Heroes who are calling in that white privilege refund and taking reparations seriously, one crumbling cracker at a time, even if it means setting aside their beloved Non-Aggression Principal and breaking out the knives and guns in the cause of African Ascent.

"It's Black Spring up in here."

-Anonymous Prophet of the Sacred Uprising, 3/30/16

This militant volume also includes the cooning screed of T. Spoone Slickens as an example of traitorous snitcherdation.

Books by James LaFond

Nonfiction

The Fighting Edge, 2000

The Logic of Steel, 2001

The First Boxers, 2011

The Gods of Boxing, 2011

All Power Fighting, 2011

When You're Food, 2011

The Lesser Angles of Our Nature, 2012

The Logic of Force, 2012

The Greatest Boxer, 2012

Take Me to Your Breeder, 2014

The Streets Have Eyes, 2014

Panhandler Nation, 2014

The Ghetto Grocer, 2014

American Fist, 2014

Don't Get Boned, 2014

Alienation Nation, 2014

In The Chinks of The Machine, 2014

How the Ghetto Got My Soul, 2014

Saving the World Sucks, 2014

Taboo You, 2014

The Fighting Life, 2014

Narco Night Train, 2014

Into the Mountains of Madness: in [3 volumes], 2014

Incubus of Your Sacred Emasculation, 2014

Breeder's Digest, 2014

The Third Eye, 2015

Modern Agonistics, 2015

By the Wine Dark Sea, 2015

The Pale Usher, 2016

The End of Masculine Time, 2015

War Drums, 2015

A Thousand Years in His Soul: The Poets, 2015

A Thousand Years in His Soul: The Seers, 2015

Of Lions and Men, 2015

Your Trojan Whorse, 2016

On Bitches, 2016

Equidistant Drowning Babies, 2015

The Boned Zone, 2015

A Sickness of the Heart: Part One, 2015

Let the Weak Fall, 2015

If I Were King, 2015

Dark Art of an Aryan Mystic, 2015

Welcome to Harm City: White Boy, 2015

When You're Food: Raw, 2016

No B.S. Boxing, 2016

Stick Fighting Fundamentals, 2016

Our Captain, 2016

Stillbirth of A Nation, 2016

America in Chains, 2106

40,000 Years from Home, 2016

The Sardonyx Stone, 2016
Neanderthal Resistance, 2016
A Dread Grace, 2016
Habitat Hoodrat, 2016
The Poor Tour/Ghetto Gourmet, 2016
40,000 Years from Home, 2016
A Once Great Medieval City, 2016
A Thousand Years in His Soul, 2016
The Liver-Eater Reader, 2016
Why Grownups Suck, 2016

Fiction
Astride the Chariot of Night, 2014
Sacrifix, 2014
Rise, 2014
Motherworld, 2014
Planet Buzzkill, 2014
Fruit of The Deceiver, 2014
Forty Hands of Night, 2014
Black and Pale, 2014
Daughters of Moros, 2014
Darkly, 2014
This Design is Called Paisley, 2015
Hurt Stoker, 2015
Poet, 2016
Triumph, 2015
Winter, 2015
The Spiral Case, 2015
Hemavore, with Dominick Mattero, 2016
Yusuf of the Dusk, 2016
Beyond the Pale, 2016

RetroGenesis: Day 1, with Erique Watson, 2015
Easy Chair, 2015
Happily Ever Under, 2015
Road Killing, 2015
Fat Girl Dancing, 2015
Buzz Bunny, 2015
T. Spoone Slickens, Inquire, 2015
Dream Flower, 2015
The Song of Jeannot, 2015
Organa, 2015
A Hoodrat Halloween, 2015
Buzz Bunny, 2015
The Consultant, 2015
Reverent Chandler, 2015
He, 2016
Little Feet Going Nowhere, 2016
DoomFawn, 2016
The Jericho Bone, 2016
Ire and Ice, 2016
Under the Crescent, 2016

Sunset Saga Novels
Big Water Blood Song, 2011
Ghosts of the Sunset World, 2011
Beyond the Ember Star, 2012
Comes the Six Winter Night, 2012
Thunder-Boy, 2012
The World is Our Widow, 2013
Behind the Sunset Veil, 2013
Den of The Ender, 2013
God's Picture Maker, 2014
Out of Time, 2015
Seven Moons Deep, 2016

Contents

Black Spring
The Baltimore County Race Purge: 2016

© 2016 James LaFond

Since late April 2015, white folks on foot have been relentlessly preyed upon by packs of black men and youth, wielding handguns, knives, bottles, bats, gas cans and lighters, stones and tree limbs. The epicenter of this violence is the Golden Ring Wal-Mart, where most people refuse to be caught on foot at night, with Wal-Mart employees avoiding the bus stops. In 2014 and 2015 this Wal-Mart had the highest crime rate of all Wal-Marts worldwide.

The Warriors of African Ascent that have hunted the Baltimore County neighborhoods of Rosedale, Essex, White Marsh and Middle-River over this past year have recently moved out from Baltimore City, and have brought with them the methods of aggression that made Baltimore the model Purge City in America in 2015, even as Baltimore County Police have shifted their attention away from Essex to the more affluent Towson precinct.

Eastern Baltimore County is undergoing a black-on-white suburban race purge. This Social Justice Initiative has been engineered by local, state and federal agencies, will hopefully eradicate the last vestiges of lingering white privilege in the purge zone and will serve as a model for suburban race purges to come.

Welcome to Harm County East.

'Up In Here'
On the #55 Line: 10:23-55 p.m. 3/30/16

© 2016 James LaFond

The #55 line spans the Towson, Parkville and Essex police precincts of Baltimore County.

The major transfer points for the #55 line in Baltimore city are all along Northern Parkway, at McClean, Harford, and Belair Roads. Crime has gotten so bad at Harford that the stop is rarely used at night, with one or none boarding, as opposed to the previous half dozen.

The driver is hitting fifty MPH, zooming through the city portion of the route, so I have to step out and get his attention. The front of the bus is occupied by 4 tough looking white guys, all of whom will offload in Overlea.

White women no longer use this bus at night and the men do not risk Rosedale or Essex stops. Hispanics and Asians are now absent. The middle portion of this bus is occupied by as many working black adults, headed home. The back deck is occupied by a pack of wannabe-Gs, posing in thuggish style, most still in their teens.

Overlea Station is under construction, temporarily safe at night, lit up by road crew lights and milling with Hispanic hardhats. As the whites offload one by one, the older black man driving gets more and more nervous, the boys in the back making fun of him, talking shit, one of them saying, "Fuck you, Old-school Nigger. It's Black Spring up in here."

Black men are threatening someone at Kenwood Plaza, the first major County transfer point, which has recently been overrun by hoodlums and thugs from the adjacent Cedonia area of the City, which is linked to the infamous Mondawmin area by the #5 line.

Right in White Time

At Golden Ring one older black woman offloads, no one loads. On Monday it was a single black man offloading. People do not risk standing on Philadelphia Road at Golden Ring.

By the time I get to the major transfer point at Stemmer's Run and Old Eastern Avenue, all that is left are the thugs on the back deck, talking shit about me, with comments such as, "Yo, Pops thinks he's walkin' dis shit?"

I am rude to the driver, and do not give him a courteous goodbye, like the other whites did. The more courteous I am to him, the greater the chance is that I get tracked back into the park. Like Monday night, as I offload with a woman, who has a man waiting for her, I notice three knots of blacks packed up defensively and eying me with misgivings. Only myself and the larger black men walk away from this mass transit hub—which has not seen a police officer after dark, for a year—alone, the rest of the blacks being met by friends, cabs, sedans or hacks, or packing up together as they offload.

I walk off into the night, out Old Eastern Avenue, the final stretch of the 2-mile two lane main artery that parallels its wider counterpart, Eastern Boulevard from Middlesex Shopping Center to Middle River Bridge, where they merge. As I consider the fact that three black-on-white attacks have occurred in the past five days, on Old Eastern Avenue, that I know of, the genius of this suburban invasion strikes me.

The #23 line, which intersects here, has brought thousands of welfare families from the Edmonson Village area of West Baltimore, where white and black elites would like to re-acquire some of the impressive early 20th century single family homes. No less than three sprawling low rise housing projects dot the end of the #23 line around Fox Ridge, with the walkway over the 702 highway having to be encased in steel to prevent bricks from being dropped on white motorists headed to their waterfront housing.

The #24 line dead ends below Cedonia, in one of the most crime ridden section of East Baltimore, where aggressive gentrification is underway, with two low rise projects having been demolished over the past 10 years. This section of East Baltimore is sitting up against three interstate highways and is being sought by developers who wish to market highway access for Washington D.C. commuters. The violent youth being moved out of Cedonia are being resettled in the Whispering Woods housing projects in Rural Carol Island, where ghetto hair salons have popped up and increasing incidents of gun and knife violence are transforming the crimescape. The #24 line runs until 1 a.m., which is a bizarre schedule for an extended secondary line, as if the MTA planners considered the needs of drug mules and assassins when this line from nowhere to nowhere was established.

Out Philadelphia Road to White Marsh runs the #35 line, which brings in crime from hyper-violent Southwest Baltimore. White Marsh Mall and The Avenue at White Marsh have been Baltimore County commercial centerpieces for decades, but are now becoming high crime zones, with the same trends as seen in Essex, Rosedale and Middle River, two or more black youth, often armed with a firearm, attacking individual white males and white couples. One wonders if the weapons used in this crime were part of the 100,000 dollars in missing merchandize from the Golden Ring Wal-Mart guns and ammo department in 2015.

These two City gentrification initiatives are propelling the resettlement of many of the most violent blacks in Baltimore City, into the adjacent County, where working class whites fled to out of East Baltimore three decades ago. Eastern Baltimore County is where working people who could not afford to buy in distant Harford County fled to in their quest to live free of rampant crime and racist mob aggression.

Black Spring is the story of the government-sponsored ghettoization of four Eastern Baltimore County communities, and of the ongoing, declared, low-intensity, black-on-white race war that has been hot since the last week of April, 2015.

A Shopping Cop
Rescues a Middle-aged Labrat from a Prime Hoodrat at the Author's Place of Employment

© 2016 James LaFond

At ten minutes to eight last Friday night, a couple of hours before the start of my shift, as my boss, Mister Ron, was unloading the truck, he was called to the front of the store. He found the Baltimore City Cop who flies the police chopper out of Martins Airport—where my dear Uncle Bernie polishes the wing tips of the Korean Conflict vintage F-86 saber jet— with an oppressed hero of the uprising against white privilege held in his cruel power, bound like Kunta Kintai himself.

Ron recognized this fellow, as a regular overnight customer, a black man in his mighty prime. This prime buck—sick and tired of being forced to work in Donald trump's tobacco sheds—had understandably attacked a white customer, some twenty years his senior, a man nearing sixty. The assault had transpired on the sidewalk outside, resulting in the younger, more colorfully blessed man beating up the older paleface, who obstinately continued to refuse to acknowledge the mastery of our hero of African ascent.

The heroic purger then drew a pocket knife and threatened the unarmed, older man, which got the attention of an evil functionary of the white oppressor state, who was off duty and out of bounds and who shamelessly arrested and held the hero of this story until uniformed goons from Baltimore County were dispatched to collect him for official persecution.

The former white privileged inflictor of racial oppression did enter the store and ask Ron for a copy of the video for use in court. Hopefully this means that our latter day Nat Turner is going to turn the tables on that sneaky white devil—who intentionally held back from punching just so our Hero would take all of the heat—and file counter charges.

Now that one of our warriors have fallen into chains it is incumbent upon another of our number to rise up and throw off these four hundred years of wicked lies—and whooping some white ass while you're at it cain't hurt, brutha!

'The Warrior Gene'
Stefan Molyneux Marshals an Army of Stats on the Real Master Race

© 2016 James LaFond

"If poverty caused crime, monks would be criminals."

-Stefan Molyneux

After seeing how much better blacks score on all of these crime bar graphs, I don't want to hear anymore about white people being the master race. Move over cracker, Tyron's moving on up—zoom—right by you, son!

Notes

1. Unreported violent crime would be much higher on the black and Hispanic side if there were not so much underreporting of crime from those dark quarters.

2. My own study of violence has indicated that entitlement—and the emotional belief in social debt—is the prime driver of violence.

3. Also, the low incidence of rape among Asians may well be due to their men being poorly equipped for the deed—just saying.

4. At 23 minutes one study out of Britain indicates [in my opinion] that women raising boys is the root cause of violent criminality.

5. Where Stefan sees these trends as unintended consequences, I believe they are the intended consequences of policies intended to eradicate masculinity, free will and spirituality.

6. The low IQ-violence correlation is reflective of physical force being an inferior method of getting what you want when compared to manipulative means. Genghis Khan would agree, as he generally packed less manpower than his enemies, but won through his wits and the discipline of his men.

7. The warrior gene information is fascinating.

8. Interestingly, Native Americans usually fielded superior warriors to their white enemies and usually thought that the whites were crazy for beating their children, and that white soldiers acted like domesticated animals rather than warriors.

9. The spanking rates by race are not as large as one would think. However, what is spanking among whites and Asians is, among blacks, punching, flogging, whipping and kicking, acts which the word spanking simply masks.

https://www.youtube.com/watch?v=TVBJ5m3sGfk&list=PLMNj_r5bccUyulYsatrzNGIvasrOeBy_Y&index=11

Pigs Huffing and Puffing
And Blowing Down Suburban Doors: 5:11 a.m., 3/31/16, Stemmer's Run & Old Eastern Ave.

I stood this morning a mile and a half from dense subsidized housing that is home to the hoodlums that hunt us mass transit users along this un-policed stretch of Old Eastern Avenue. By unpoliced I mean that patrol officers are no longer seen cruising by providing a deterrent. We do see the occasional speeding squad car with lights blaring, heading somewhere else. But the cops no longer linger where the street crime is, but are involved in more pressing concerns such as bringing in revenue via traffic tickets and also in fighting the drug war.

At 5:11 this morning a dark, unmarked car with blacked out windows cruised through the intersection with an SUV five feet behind it, its windows blocked out, rumbling along in the dark, headed across Old Easter on Stemmers Run where it turns into Turkey Neck Road, and merges with Highway 702 almost a mile down the road. These cops—federal, state, local, martian—are headed into a blooming ghetto, an opiate rose strangling the working people who are being hunted increasingly on the street, in their driveways and in their houses, with home invasions on the upswing, and being falsely reported as robberies and burglaries.

At 5:19 a caravan rumbles through the light at ten miles per an hour in the wake of the two porkmobiles. There are about ten vehicles, five feet apart, shaking the road surface: an unmarked SUV, a big rumbling pickup truck, two armored fighting vehicles that seem to hold six tactical cops each, an Emergency Medical Services van, an ambulance, the rest of the vehicles an assortment of unmarked cops cars.

Like the City, six miles south and west, when police activity is devoted to fight the drug war, the traditional deterrence role is reduced, with the police now limited to documenting the crime they are stretched too thin to deter. The belief that junkies are robbing and beating folks to pay for their habit when an area is ghettoized, is false, as is the claim that busting drug dealers will stop recreational mob attacks and hate-fueled beatings, when in fact addicts shoplift, beg, work and prostitute themselves for their drugs.

Who is attacking people at and near these bus stops at night?

According to the police blotter the attackers are identical, genderless, "unknown-suspects."

At some point this summer I'll find out.

'Some Respect for Pigs?'

A Plea from Joel for Solidarity in the Face of Black Spring

© 2016 James LaFond

"As the cousin of a police officer I do feel a twinge of regret when I read the term 'Pig' in your posts. Based on the fact that your 'black heroes' are hunting you in Harm City, and apparently now in Harm County as well, I would think that you might side with your allies-of-circumstance in blue. Come on, James, could we show some respect for 'pigs?'"

-Joel

Absolutely, Joel. The Pigs deserve recognition. They are, after all engaging in a war of sorts and that takes a certain amount of positive qualities. In fact, I think the Baltimore County Cops deserve an anthem as they fight the hero-storm that is the Black Spring Uprising.

So, for pigs fighting the drug war, what better anthem could there be but...

https://www.youtube.com/watch?v=K3b6SGoN6dA

https://www.youtube.com/watch?v=9ssDXiMLX9o

PS: If you're a pig and you don't like this guy, feel better, because my friend Raphael and three other Puerto Rican meatheads beat his ass when they were working security at one of these concerts and found him walking round mumbling back stage, not even speaking a language they could identify as English.

A Pink Assault Rifle

Father and Son Martyred by Caucasian Occupation Troops at Green Mount Cemetery

© 2016 James LaFond

"A nice guy who was getting his act together and going back to school" and his father pulled up in the 400 block of East Lavalle Street on April Fool's Day, strapped, locked and loaded to put some stitches in some snitches. Unfortunately for our Black Spring heroes three cops from a tactical unit were rolling up on some other business. Upon seeing the young man with the handgun and the father with the scooped, pink assault rifle taking aim at some rival "players in the game" the cops, with out even taking a moment to consider that the father might have been involved in a breast cancer awareness initiative, "lit dey asses up," hosing down the father and son with 56 rounds, which has community activists questioning this excessive use of force, as well as the fact that the three cracker cops did not identify themselves, shout a warning, discuss options with or otherwise advise the Fallen before opening fire.

Some white blogger had the audacity to excuse the number of rounds expended on the fact that BPD cops have to pay for their own practice ammunition—which you just know is B.S., but there you have the cover up beginning. Two neighborhood traitors claim that the cops saved some innocent children that were about to be caught in the crossfire, who were given time to scatter, as if those porch monkeys didn't already know what to do. These fools shall be dealt with.

-Justin W. R. Justice reporting for YoBlackSpring.net on this cracker atrocity up in here.

PS: Binkie, I worked ovatime on dis shit and needs to get paid—Five'O eyeballin' ma black ass da whole entire time, you feel me, Yo?

Right in White Time

ReBound's Big Play
A Black Spring Hero Tale

Saturday Night, Old Eastern Avenue, Essex

Rebound [with a capital B, nigga], sorry, ReBound and his homeboy—"who jus' gettin' wit da game en ain't up to a handle yet"—knocked on this old white bitch's door just to see if she opened it, and she did. So ReBound and his homeboy burst in and smacked her down, about ready to make shit right with some garb and go, and his homeboy said, "Yo, I jus' heard some lock en load bullshit, yo—let's get!"

They bolted outside and saw some lights and ran back down the way with nothing to show for their trouble. ReBound was still giving his homeboy shit about it on the bus, the following Wednesday, across from some Santa Claus lookin' somebody...

Black Spring Reparations 101
The Classic Bus Stop Strong-Arm Robbery

Friday Afternoon, Old Eastern Avenue and Glenwood, Essex

While waiting for the bus under the shelter a white woman was approached by an innocent, misunderstood, unarmed, victim of her oppression, who rose up against Whitey then and there, pressed her against the back of the shelter, reached his hand into her pocket, and took her wallet, which contained cash, credit cards and identification.

Prudently wishing to avoid the long, pale hand of the law, our hero fled back into the rental complex he had emerged from, having made one more bold stroke against the evil oppressor state that profited from the enslavement of his ancestors—who didn't steal shit, and you see where that got them!

Right in White Time

Thank You, John, For Your Support

I Would Like To Inform You That You Have Won A

© 2016 James LaFond

Free, all expenses paid trip to the Super-8 Motel on Route 40 in the historic Harm City neighborhood of Highlandtown. We see that you purchased *When You're Food*, and have arranged for you to be escorted via MTA bus by Mister Badshydbe Distant, who speaks all Harm City ebonic dialects fluently. When you offload at the Baltimore Travel Plaza, look for the older bald man with the pecan complexion, wearing the red fez and carrying your 1898 Boer War Era British pith helmet... Seriously, you will be the first person to test fly our interactive, online Habitat Hoodrat Travel Guide!

Congratulations, John!

Right in White Time

The Price of Privilege
Tax Time in Harm County

© 2016 James LaFond

Bill, who has squandered the rape of Mother Africa's children, by failing to live up to the gross consumption, high living and soul-driving ethos of white men of old—and appearing to have no idea that just minding his own business and getting by would do nothing to erase the sins of his race—was walking down North Marlyn Avenue, near Edmund's Way at 1:55 in the afternoon the Thursday before last.

At this time, two innocent, unarmed, good-intended, teenage victms of white privilege, were walking down Marylin, having just left the government school. These two anonymous heroes of The Uprising would have rather been at home playing with their X-Box, rapping to MTV—which some fool said used to be white channel—or macking some hos. But they stayed true to the cause and swooped down on that young-ass cracker, who forget white people were not supposed to fight back, and began trading punches. Seeing two innocent, unarmed bruthas being beaten by that evil white dude caused two more Black Spring Heroes, who were walking nearby, to charge, heroically, heedless of their own safety, to the defense of their fellows. Seeing that his one-on-two attack had now turned into a one-on four attack, the cowardly cracker turned and ran away.

No wealth was paid into the limitless well of guilt that is the reparations cause, but an effort was made on behalf of The People, and at least one violent white devil was shown that attacking black children in public will not be tolerated by the black community, because black lives matter!

Yo, Help!
A Possibly Tragic Misunderstanding

© 2016 James LaFond

5:10 a.m., Parkville, Friday, March 25

On Harford Road, a driver for an ambulatory service was pulling out from the parking lot when he was flagged down by an innocent, unarmed, young, black man. Although the innocent victim of white privilege was obviously lost or broke and in need of directions to the nearest temporary agency so that he could be first in line sign to up for the work-able program when that joint opened in three hours, the white fool driving the mobility van thought that the paper with directions on it being waved in his face was a gun.

Even though the poor dude had just opened the passenger side door to ask for directions, the driver thought this was a robbery and handed over his cellphone and wallet. Terrified now, that this misunderstanding might result in police coming down on him and jacking his ass up like Freddie Gray, the victim of this misunderstanding fled back into the neighborhood.

Is Yo Serious or Is Yo Delirious?
A Clarion Call for Bruthidarity from Justin W. R. Justice

© 2016 James LaFond

Reporting from the front lines of the war on whitey, I must stop, put my hands up, say don't shoot and then remind you retarded nigglets that y'all ain't supposed to be banking bruthas en sistas but jus' dem white devils. Nigga, how difficult can it be—they glow in the dark, Yo!

Read below—and between the lines—of the White People Times Police Blotter.

1. At 6:30 p.m. on April 1, a known suspect and four unknown suspects [meaning a nigga he knew and four niggas he didn't know] knock on the door of this bruthas' mammas' apartment while she out slaving for White Daddy, invade and beat his ass.

2. Early on that week, on the 29th, three a you young hoppers—one with a knife—run up on this young brutha en try and rob him, en he runoff

into the arms of some white store owner and those fools run off. The point is, if this had been a white boy, his slow ass would have been caught en these dude's a robbed him. But now, not only do these hoppers have to pick on a brutha, they can't catch his scared ass!

3. And last, Dillon, a brutha, even though his White Daddy-worshipping mamma named him like a white man was riding his bike home from work and three young bruthas attempt to rob him, to which he said, "I'll give you my lunch receipt. I can't even afford a bus ticket yo, and I'd appreciate keeping my I.D." So the brutha is cool about it and no harm is done. But that could have been a bagged polar bear, a successful hunt.

Y'all needs to get on the same page even though your young asses cain't read! At least stand together!

-Justin W. R. Justice

Raiding Polar Bear Dens
A Black Spring Counter-Oppression Session

First, on April 1, in Essex, we got our five young guns runnin' up in a bruthas apartment and beating his ass, and the poleese do not classify this as a home invasion, which it is, but as an assault. As tragic as this shit is there is a lesson there.

Second—but first, chronologically speaking—on March 29, we have a young brutha run up in some old white bitch's house over in Parkville, wrestle with her, in her house, and run off with her purse, and the poleese report it as a robbery, when it should be reported as a home invasion.

Third, on April 1, over in Parkville, another young brutha runs up in a white lady's house, while she is home and just takes her purse and again the poleese do not report it for what it is.

Now the poleese have no love for black folks, let alone for members of the Black Spring New African Uprising, but the poleese are afraid—

more than anything—of white people with guns. White people with guns could actually kick the ass of the poleese, en they know it. So, in order to keep white people—who read, unlike your trifling asses—from getting worried and start buying guns and defending their houses, by reporting home invasions for what they are, they downplay that shit. This is a signal to Black Spring to move indoors and catch those polar bears hibernating in their dens!

Now, below is a cautionary tale about Golds, which just happened on April 2, in Essex, at the epicenter of our militancy.

Now Golds goes into this white people house— one of those real nice, I got a lot a shit and done forgot we gettin' real up in the hood now joints—while they three polar bear asses go out on they boat. Golds loots that joint. Now Golds breaks into that joint at 11:45 p.m. on Saturday, stacks their shit up and kicks back to enjoy they liquor and TV, and that fine couch—which his dumbass falls asleep on. Now what do you think happens while he's laying there dreaming 'bout selling all they shit and getting'a gold grille on his teeth?

That's right, the three polar bears are on their way home!

At 11:45 on Sunday morning, ten hours after his ass should have been gone, he wakes up on the coach with Mamma polar bear screaming at his ass. A course she just some white bitch so he goes after her. But then, lo and take hold, with Mamma polar bear and Baby polar bear standing by, old Papa Polar Bear runs Gold's ass out of there, leaving all of his fancy polar bear shit he was going to sell for that gold grille still back up in there.

Let that be a lesson to you lazy uprisers!

Meanwhile, while Golds is sleeping off his polar bear juice drunk, some other drunk homeboy is shooting at fellow colored folk at the S& S Lounge at Overlea Station. Brutha, what is wrong with you! There are hundreds of white households within a mile of that joint!

Get with it now.

Come to the night.

On the other hand, over there in Parkville, Davontay is getting' shit done the old fashioned way, sticking guns in palefaces and taking they shit out on the street the way it was meant to be!

Overall, setting the tone on the street and keeping those polar bears locked down in their dens is preferable. That way, you can choose to raid whatever den you like, and the poleese, if they do get involved, will classify it as a robbery or assault, or some other bullshit, all to our just cause though they racist asses don't know it not.

Keeping if real, if not ideal, from the Black Spring Uprising Front Line, Justin W. R. Justice

The Soul Saga of Shabazmataz Murphy

Justin W. R. Justice Reporting on the Martyrfication of an Arab/Black Spring Hero

© 2016 James LaFond

It was bad enough that his mamma named him Shabaz, hoping he'd become a Black Muslim. It was a simple enough fix, for one wanted to continue eating barbecued pork rinds and drinking malt liquor, to hiphopify that handle to Shabazmataz.

But then what to do with a young oppressed life under the heel of White Privilege?

Everyone knows that you can't get ahead with Whitey standing on your neck.

Why not become a Yo-Gee-Oh collectable card player—a regular shark of the nerd arena?

There were only one—well two—problems: the Japanese company that made these collectable playing cards rigmitized them decks. The white Nazis might have their trickanometry, but the

Japanese have their rigmatization, which is a way of cheating by having so many rules for new cards that a brother doesn't have a chance of locking that stuff down in the brain before them Asian kids hijacked that joint. This just added to his stigmatization.

So, Shabazmataz Murphy—at least named after the onetime President of Baltimore—decided to level the playing field.

At 3:54 p.m., Saturday, April 9, in Year One of the Uprising, at the Caroll Island Walmart, Shabazmataz reparated 11 decks of cards, whereupon he was approached by two evil, racist, white, Nazi enforcers, intent on preventing him from obtaining the same number of trading cards as that funky smelling Pakistani kid whose father owns the liquor store. These two crackers thought they were going to lay some more oppression on our man, but he was busting through, as big as both of their narrow asses combined. He shoved both of them, but then realized that that trickanometry had come into play against him as well, for these Nazi enforcers were strong as shit, obviously bred on some white supremacy steroid farm—and down he go!

Shabazmataz was rigmatized, stigmatized and soon pygmatized when the poleese showed up!

Ghost Bus
Homeboy Apocalypse Update

© 2016 James LaFond

I have been taking the 9:23 bus ever since the April 2016 Race Purge, instead of the 10:23 bus. The 9:23 has about half of the previous passengers, the route never having recovered from the purge. The corner of Northern and Harford at Valentino's Restaurant, is not even used after dark anymore. Last night I over slept. It was a beautiful, mild spring night out, the kind of night that is a predictor of moderately heavy bus traffic. I was, however, surprised that only one other passenger was on the last #55 of the night. He is an older black man dressed like a retail manager, who gets off at Golden Ring, where most people will not risk using the stops.

This bus used to load up with 25 people between Towson and Hamilton and then head out through Overlea and Rosedale to Essex, with many of the passengers making the whole ride. Although the Towson and Hamilton passengers were absent, five souls did board at lonely, darkened stops—not one at a major transfer point—as these areas are hunted by black thug mobs that attack whites, blacks, Latinos and Asians with roughly equal frequency.

Who gets on the bus?

- An Indian or Pakistani kid

- A black woman

- A black couple

- A black woman who works at the Hospital and who I based the Kendra character on in Planet Buzzkill

Only Kendra stays on for the final leg into Essex, where thousands of Baltimore City ghetto-dwellers have been moved with housing vouchers over the past five years. It is interesting that hard working black folks have suffered the most from the government-sponsored spread of unemployed criminals and welfare children into outlying areas of Baltimore. It is doubly interesting that the championing of the cause of black criminals and the pressure on police to back off of these people has hurt working blacks far more than any other group. Of the aporoximately30 regular commuters who I no longer see on this bus since last year's purge, 25 were black.

Where are they?

They are paying more to get to work, most likely, by employing cabs, sedans, Uber drivers or hacks. Major transfer points in Hamilton, Overlea, Rosedale, Essex and Middle River are now rarely occupied by commuters after dark.

Never fear, though, as I walked out to Middle River I saw the first police car on patrol along Old Eastern Avenue—which is now a hot zone for muggings, stickups and home invasions—in 12 months. The pig didn't bother cruising down the street, but just sat at the 7-11. It was an oddly quiet night, with little light from the half moon. Even my friend, the giant egret, was not standing proudly out in the water beneath the bridge, but had hunched over at the edge of the reeds

I like the solitude and suppose I owe the white, liberal slave masters for letting their moral chattel loose on those who had previously escaped their clutches, thereby clearing the night for my ongoing mediation on the marginal meaning of human life.

I savored the quiet night.

Mandingo Bingo Winner off the Hook

Justin W. R. Justice Reporting from the Halls of Injustice

© 2016 James LaFond

A Baltimore City School Poleese who was caught red-handed on video slapping an innocent, unarmed victim of White Privilege on March 1, has won the Mandingo Bingo sweepstakes, in which our White Mommy occasionally feels sorry for some Uncle Tom type. However, he was still a grown-ass man whooping a chyle—which some evil Nazi so-in-so went so far as to call hoodrat handball.

Hoodrat Handball!

Now—and let you young militants listen up—this brutal poleese still face two misdemeanor charges so is not completely off the hook. Notice in the video below what a masterful job the young brutha does slyly filming this act of oppression and note how perfect it was and could have been, except for the fact that our hero spit on this big poleese in front of the female cop.

Little brutha, you got to be slicker than that!

Just like the cameraman does not start his clip until after the spit, don't spit into you are out of sight of that deputized clit, keeping in mind, that if she not there—it's on and after he lays them first hits in you don't want to be caught under his big ass, so you best run like old Koon-Ta-Kunt-Ay lighting out from Master's plantation.

Look, it is a sure thing to bring on a poleese ass whoopin' if you spit on them. So—especially considering how big his George Foreman-looking self was—it was a brave thing, but ill-advised so long as the female cop was there. Now, if you hung like Terrence White, then maybe you can have female cops lying for you. However, barring that unlikely anatomical circumstance, you need to do this shit on the sly when no witnesses sympathetic to him are around. For instance, you could have set this up in the boys room. Use your imagination, Yo and the pants leg is not the limit.

https://www.youtube.com/watch?v=N432rbvCeyo

The Three Little People
When the Hoodrat Wolf-Pack Huffs and Puffs and Threatens to Blow Your Door In

© 2016 James LaFond

Yesterday, at 5:30 p.m., I was headed up to the gym, cutting through the Ridgely Oak neighborhood, when, walking up White Oak to Oak, I saw a group of 20-30 older teen and adult blacks, evenly mixed between male and female. I noticed the males as I was behind and they were the support element. The victims and neighbors noticed the females.

I had a friend check on social media with the neighborhood association and have a rough understanding of what transpired before and after I made a right up Oak and passed a county pig cruising toward the scene. Currently this neighborhood is only 15% black, yet they own the streets as the sissy whites wonder what is happening. The social media posts indicate a total incomprehension of black urban culture. The media has prepped these victims well.

I do not know if the specific victims were white, and based on media posts, am guessing that they are not, because they seemed to know what was what, unlike the neighbors who were shocked. If they were white or black does not matter. If decent blacks move into your neighborhood and you do not have men to defend them from the gangs that will root them out so that they can be your residential predators, then you are next.

The daughter has been subject to attacks at school and has been pulled from Loch Raven Senior High.

The predators Googled her house address and showed up in masse to stage a home invasion, led by an adult woman. These teen males were on average six feet and 180 pounds.

The parents were at work.

The rest of the information is hazy.

The two grandfathers showed up to defend the house, apparently unarmed. One was stricken down and four mob members breached the front door and were able to lay hands on the girl.

Police arrived, with one cop falling on the sidewalk as the mob fled.

Police and neighbors are suggesting assault charges, where this was clearly a blatant home invasion.

I have, in the past, been in this situation.

If you are in this situation do not open your door to communicate with the besiegers. Moral authority does not apply to mob attacks.

If you must open the door to retrieve a family member do not do so unarmed and do not rely on a blunt weapon, which is of limited value against a mob. Appear with an edged weapon or firearm, making sure to advance only enough to bring in your kin. Do not attempt to drive off the besiegers. Such sorties are frowned on by the Police State, which is first and foremost concerned with the rights of your attackers and the prospect of you using a weapon.

Get back inside as soon as possible. If the cops see you on the lawn with a weapon, you may be one of the roughly 500 whites killed by cops this year as opposed to the approximately 200 blacks killed by cops in the same period of occupation.

If you have two men, the strong one should hold the door and push back, while the other uses a weapon—such as a butcher knife or fireplace poker—on whatever attacker manages to breach the open portion of the door.

This is why sensible city dwellers, when hunkering down, always install barred security storm doors that open outward and have heavy inside doors that open toward a wall that your back can be braced against while your partner butchers those hoodrats who squeeze through to get their huminary cheese.

Note that this is a suburb that working and middle class city folks resettled to when they were driven from Baltimore decades ago. The State is now sending their moral chattel across the DeYoified Zone to root at the children of those who escaped.

Below is the link to a house listed for sale within two blocks of the attack. There are multiple sale signs on every block. The tide has risen and the inner dykes are breached. The fight will now be house to house.

This was a Black Spring Tactical Strike in one of the Baltimore County neighborhoods I am studying as the hunt for palefaces and colored sympathizers intensifies. Do note that the neighborhood association was told by the police that they do not always have "the resources" to send out an officer on such calls. The cops seem to be using a counter-surge strategy.

https://www.coldwellbankerhomes.com/md/baltimore/8529-oak-road/pid_11508646/

Afterward

The felons have announced that they will be back and know well that the police can not provide protection. The commentary by the local whites about how the adult female was setting a bad example show astounding ignorance. That bitch was setting a good example, training up a click on behalf of some other, more influential, woman operating behind the scenes. She is probably the aunt of one of the attackers.

Rudyard
An Uber Driver Wonders Outloud

Last night I took this call in Owings Mills—a good area, out of the city by many miles. When I arrive at the pickup location the client calls and wants me to pick him up across the street from the designated pickup. I complied.

The man was young and of tremendous stature, a black man. His hands were larger than my head, his arms twice the girth of my legs and he was angry. He thanked me for picking him up at his changed location and then began to rant about the previous Uber driver declining to change locations and driving off. Now that he was inside of my car—which tilted from the burden—and I regarded his great size, I began to reconsider my agreement to alter the pickup location.

I was further disturbed—and began to further question my own judgment in this matter—when I heard his conversation, for he was on his smart phone the entire trip, as we headed into the City, to an area where I would have been none to likely to pick him up. I thought then as to the probable outcome of a disagreement with this man and the likely ending did not bode well for me, not at all.

As we went upon our way his attention thankfully turned from his displeasure with the Uber service to his own concerns, which were aired in troubling detail in my back seat. His manner was menacing. His tone was more so. However, the substance of his "business" and his willingness to discuss these things within my hearing filled me with dread. I tell you, sir, I was in fear for my life. This was a man that one does not cross, and who is errant enough in his dealings that one might never truly know if they be crossing him until it is too late. What kind of person conducts themselves with such menacing audacity. I thought to myself?

The answer need not be spoken among worldly men, of course.

In any event the service was rendered and he seemed to forget me as soon as he left the vehicle, for which I am grateful and which I trust remains the case. This and other questionable passengers this week have me wondering as to the viability of driving for

Uber. It is better than driving under some other circumstances, surely. But the question remains, is the world any longer a place where one can expose themselves in their daily business to such a variety of people and expect to return home to his family?

In my home country of Nigeria, there are many such bad sorts of fellows. To be certain they might infest any country. But there—and in most places in the world—they are in their bad places, their enclaves, their slums, their tribal compounds, not standing beside a hotel frequented by good people in an outlying suburb. Why this is madness!

I nodded my agreement.

Counterfeit Cops
Are These Fake Pigs or Military Contractors?

© 2016 James LaFond

I have been in and out of the house on this bucolic spring day listening to my black neighbors talking about "the roaches [criminals] coming out."

Every half hour there is a police car roaring around Hamilton with its siren blaring—there goes one right now, at 4.57, up White venue, making my window frames shake. For the past six months I have rarely seen a police cruiser that has not had its lights on thundering somewhere in a hurry. Part of this—most of it, I think—is that fact that cops do not have the community support, or even the ideal of it, to answer calls one or two at a time. Every asshole that needs cuffed now tales five cops, a t least, due to the threat of legal action on behalf of the Oppressed Brethren of Martyr Gray.

An hour and a half ago, right after I glared at the Nods—a local family of heroin addicts—I saw an ambulance, a pumper truck and a cruiser flying off to the north. Cops no longer do anything alone but converge in packs of screaming cruisers, so I was surprised to see another cop car lazily make the turn in the wrong direction, not the least bit concerned about where his colleagues were off to and why. This car turns off of Hamilton onto Harford in the southbound lane within three paces of where I stood counting my money on the curb in front of Hamilton Liquors.

Something did not add up:

There were two pigs in this cruiser, both black, and they seemed to have full tactical gear on minus the helmet. The passenger was slouching like some gangster and talking into his radio as if to a girlfriend or homeboy, not police business. An air of lazy unprofessional contempt hung upon the two uniformed men as they smiled and cruised.

The car was a blue and white but was kind of big and old for a BPD cruiser.

There was a sheriff's emblem around police, with the municipality markings removed.

The cops had no BPD insignia that I could see and seemed to have a slightly darker shade of blue uniform than the norm.

Who were these faggots?

Why are they here?

Why did a regular BPD cruiser speed by them with its lights on and not stop and pull into reverse and ask these jokers what the hell they were doing in Baltimore City?

Where did these faggots come from?

Rolling One Deep
An Hour in the Life of an Aggression Cipher

© 2016 James LaFond

Today I walked down into Cedonia to have a look around, checking for tell-tale ground litter and other signs of dire times. I stopped at the Sunny Mart and caught a news bit about the conviction and sentencing of a handful of the pack of hoodrats who stamped an older East Baltimore man into a coma this time last year. The 15-year-old girl who stomped on his head while he was already in a coma got 15 irony-laced years. She will be out when she's 30, a hardened murderess of some 300 pounds...

2:30 p.m.

I checked the spot where the four boys tried to blitz me late last summer at night and am now convinced that I moved further and faster than I thought I did. I had an immediate memory of darting across the intersection of Mary and Greenhill and getting my back against a working van while I pulled out my shank. It seems to me that that van was parked right on the corner. But the thing has always been parked fifty feet past the corner every time I've gone by since, so I think I was suffering from stress-induced spatial distortion. This bipedal lab is loads of fun. I'll miss it when it final gets scrapped.

https://www.redfin.com/MD/Baltimore/4610-Mary-Ave-21206/home/10352452

While I was pacing this out, a 20-year-old black fellow in a neat blue polo shirt and bare head cruised by in a blue 2014BMW, really revving the engine as if ready to peel off fast, but only rushing down the street at about 25 mph as he looked intently into yards and lots.

He circled this block three times in succession, with a one-minute interval in between each.

He then sped off.

After he was gone for 10 minutes and I began walking back to Hamilton I noticed the BPD chopper banking high over head and doing an oval pattern around me. then, as I walked down Mary, passed the white van that I seem to have much affinity for, including the fact that it is injured, with a duct-taped mirror hanging off the door frame, I noticed two cop cars have Kavon—an alley with a road's name—at the bottom of the hill.

I do not know what that was about, or even if those three observations of activity were in any way connected. The police and fore sirens are screaming again, the chopper is banking off the southeast, and I'm wondering if there never will be another riot, another purge—if the sacred unrest is behind us and that maybe we are simply living in a new urban order now?

Comments

» Add a comment «
Ronald   April 21, 2016 5:26 PM EDT

James in 2007 right there were you are talking about by lehmen hardware there was a 6 packs liquor store which I stopped by to you guessed it to buy a 6 pack I just got off from a night shift job when I was in the store their was a shooting out side my truck which I had only 6 months had a side window shot out and the tire shot I called 911 the cops didn't have time to make me a report so I could give it to the insurance company the next day I had to call 911 3 time before I could get a report

'Hard-Edged Views on Race'
City Paper's Wandering Eye by Vanilla Smith

© 2016 James LaFond

This link is from a while back and was just sent to me by a local reader. I find it fascinating that a white liberal would even give me this much press. The caveat is a must if they want to keep their writing gig. And yes, I was targeted for death by a platform member of BASH Baltimore Area Skin Heads in the late 1980s, who hired 4 members of the Wasted Youth Belair-Eddison street gang to do me in—upon which the idiots got high, stabbed the wrong guy, who beat them up, and then were sent respectively to the hospital and to prison, where they where those two were dealt with by Aryan Brotherhood members, who also hated me for giving preferential hiring to blacks and firing whites, but decided not to do me in because I was a breeding white who stayed with his wife and child and all their daddies had left their mommies...

Check out the all-surveying eye of the bleeding heart of the Left via the link below.

http://www.citypaper.com/blogs/the-news-hole/bcp-wandering-eye-videos-from-baltimores-own-blackbrunch-protests-the-hardedged-views-on-race-from-one-b-20150109-story.html

'Without an Address'
You Will Be Un-Avenged by the Police

© 2016 James LaFond

I love how Colin researches social media and other idiocy associated with the videos he posts.

All I have to say is that if I were a young black guy I would be hunting white hipsters and yuppies all year long! We need much more liberal white slaughter.

Really, as a Darwinist, am I really supposed to get behind these white faggots!

Yo, Duquantay, get dat one—the one with the patches on da elbows of his grandma's sweater! Bank 'is ass!

https://www.youtube.com/watch?v=7JIFwj9kfFU

Comments

» Add a comment «
PRCD   April 24, 2016 7:49 PM EDT

The seduction of appeasement. On some other site, I read that now we're paying criminals not to commit crime. It's working as long as you don't report the crimes the paid criminals do, in fact, commit.

This will keep happening until we hit another 60s-80s-style crime wave. This time, there is a lot less social cohesion and a lot more diversity, so it should be a lot more interesting!

'I'm Not Tryin' Ta Go Ta Jail'
A Friday Afternoon in Harm County at the Dawn of Black Spring

© 2016 James LaFond

Last Friday, as I left the school at the corner of Joppa and Loch Raven in scenic Baltimore County, and stepped away from the door facing Pastore's Deli across Loch Raven, I was feeling pretty good, having sparred with a law enforcement client for over a half hour. The right eye is so bad now from two boxing lifetimes of getting hit that I must always have sunglasses on in the sunlight. Even so, I was feeling fist-proof, as my younger, taller, quicker fighter had only laid a glove on me twice.

Then, in my line of sight, the veritable picture of sloth emerged from within the tiny moral space he had previously occupied in the crack between the concrete walk and the curb...

He was forty-years-old, nearly black, with a slight paunch, sunken chest and glossy complexion, wearing black cargo shorts and a tight, sky blue T-shirt. He immediately homed in on me, with his slavish panhandling posture, his head arching low on his pigeon neck as he said, in an African accent, "Excuse me, sir, I'm not tryin' ta go ta jail."

[Translation: If you do not give me what I want I am willing to commit a crime to attain my ends, even if it means an arrest and possible criminal conviction]

I stepped around him as he turned, stopped, cracking into a broad grin as I took off my sunglasses, the sun now to my back, savoring the implicit threat, awaiting its consummation.

He then backed up against the other wall of the corner as I closed with him with the sun to my back. His tune then changed, "I'm not sayin' I'd go ta jail on you, sir—I got a daughter, need food and clothes. Please, sir, help me stay outta jail, 'cause I gotta do what I gotta do to put clothes on her back and food on da table, sir."

I stepped up to him and said, "I'm broke—get paid tomorrow. Sorry. Good luck."

I then replaced the sunglasses and walked down to the liquor store with him following me. I walked in past a pack of hoodrats, two of whom marked me to the tallest. The man did not follow but began begging a local white stoner coming out to the main drag to buy his dope.

I bought a 24-ounce can of Miller Genuine Draft and a 24-ounce can of Molson from the Puerto Rican clerk as the Russian chick stocked the shelves.

As I stepped out, I noticed the beggar and the stoner walking together, talking about something in hushed tones. There were three male hoodrats and two females. As I walked past them the two smaller ones nodded to the big one and he began to follow me, so I crossed the street. When someone follows on a walk, crossing the street is a good way to check for intent.

He stopped.

They watched me.

I stepped up on the curb across the street and pulled out my flip phone, my beer in the left hand.

He looked at them.

They nodded toward me.

He looked at me as I pretended to be fussing with my flip phone, standing there, half turned away, on the grassy strip between the sidewalk and the gutter.

As he neared me I put the phone in my pocket, sliding it past the folding knife, and cupping the knife butt between my thumb and forefinger as I turned and looked directly into his eyes.

He stopped, turned his head to look at them and they nodded "No," to which he dropped his head, looked at his feet and quick-stepped around me and headed down into the rentals.

I looked at him go, looked at them, and scanned the rest of the area before moving off.

Really, I thought they did a reasonable job of avoiding a low-yield mess.

This is how a pedestrian begins to establish his predation signature, by always remaining alert, using eye-contact and tactical positioning to control the pre-contact aspects of the encounter, and by adapting non-verbal confrontational solutions to implied threats and developing aggression.

Comments

» Add a comment «
Kman   April 27, 2016 8:37 AM EDT

James,

This story is a classic example of what Marc "the animal" McYoung refers to as " failing the intetview" phase of a street crime.

K-

SidVic   April 26, 2016 4:08 PM EDT

James,

I took a position at Uof M school of medicine in 1996. I worked on greene street. I was in Japan at the time i accepted the position and they sent me a orientation packet. I digress, but my background is strict scot-irish southern. Anyways the advice for baltimore, in this UM packet, was as follows: wear comfortable running shoes, don't carry items- keep hands free, walk close to street not buildings, telephones with direct access to security are on every block (plus they assured that if you were incapacitated that it was just necessary to get the phone out of the cradle and the cavalry would arrive!) etc etc....

I was robust young and remember laughing it off. My Jap friends were genuinely shocked and concerned. Back then i regularly regrew appendages when they gotten broken off....

Anyways, despite being a complete idiot i seldom ventured into the red zone of your map (good work on the map by the way). i did eat and park north of the market (found cheap roof lot), however. So i found occasion to travel in the red zone, sometime late. A couple of times i was on very alarmed among large group of youngish black males, but i never had any serious problems. I made eye contact and smiled broadly at all. I was surprised that northern negros seemed surly compared to those i was used to in the south (not all- some were sweet as hell).

I remember telling telling a black balto friend (he was west indies originally-they good ppl) who was quizzing me on how i found baltimore about my strategy of grinning like a fool. He laughed uproariously and told me to keep with what was working.

In retrospect, i believe that i was lucky mostly, and that my smiley demeanor was unusual enuf to keep them off me.

The Play Pen
Total Tactical Awareness in the Age of Unspoken Aggression

© 2016 James LaFond

All around the United States of Decay mobs of black youth are attacking Asians and Whites for no other cause than hateful expression. In Baltimore City and Baltimore County dispersed groups of two and three youths are beginning the great summer hunt. I have spent most of the winter and spring indoors, training and trying to publish as many books as I can before going in quest of The Liver-Eater.

Part of this effort must include a return to the mixed-race sports bar to do follow up interviews with the regulars who work in all corners of Baltimore. This means that I will be preyed upon coming and going to the bar about one out of six trips. I can halve this to 1 in 12 by picking my times carefully. Then there is the route to consider. I can go the front way or the back way.

The front way has been charted for available weapons, and I would have one within reach approximately every half block of the five. The aggression is also more confrontational and testing and less serious than what might happen going the back way through the church yard, lot and alley. However the front way will generate more encounters. I also would not want to return via the front way if harassed or marked coming down into Hamilton that way.

So the back way must be scouted, by day.

The Church yard offers numerous garden bricks.

The lot is large, unlit, has four egress points and has few handy weapons, favoring the aggressor.

In between the church yard and the lot behind the bar is a narrow walk with an oxygen supply compound behind razor wire and a thirty by twenty foot fenced in playground for the children who attend the church daycare. This is a dirt or mud compound depending on the weather and is a wonderland of boyhood. What boy does not like to build forts?

I saw one boy screaming to get back into his construction site when his hipster parents came to pick him up. This play ground has hardhats [real ones], boards, tarps, buckets and other things all strewn about. I am not in the habit of looking into the compound because I do not want the young women who work there when I do my afternoon shopping to think I am some barbarian who would make them dress up like Barbara Eden and say "Yes, Master..."

So, with election today, and with me confident that the degenerate citizens of this decaying state are fully capable of choosing the masters they deserve without my input, I walked by and stopped, taking inventory of the arsenal.

Most of the lumber is too big. Buckets don't have stopping power and the hard hats are too small. But there are four 24 inch spades, fully serviceable miniature dirt shovels that look more vicious than WWI entrenching tools. I tested the fence and was able to leap it easily enough despite my torn guts. This is my weapon cache in case I am hunted through these parts this summer. I imagine using a power-assist stroke or thrust with my stick hand gripping the steel haft right above the handle and my off hand grabbing the cross-piece of the handle in an under/over apposing grip. Access to the ribcage and brain should be a simple matter from a tight guard.

I feel much better now.

Comments

» Add a comment «

grasspunk   April 28, 2016 2:07 PM EDT

If you know your routes in advance wouldn't it be wise to redecorate them with some pretty bricks and rebar at reasonable intervals?

 **responds:** April 28, 2016 4:54 PM EDT

Wise, yes, Grasshappa, but would it be honorable.

Now, snatch the crack vile from my hand...

Surviving State-Sponsored Aggression

Black Spring Survival Guide #1

In the new Harm City Predatory Matrix which has undergone extensive improvements in methodology, since that hallowed day one year ago, when the oppressed followers' followers of Freddie "Don't-Whop-My-Ass-No-More" Grey, who rose up and said, "Hands up, don't shoot, while I beat, rob, rape and perforate these white folks" put the police in line. As a public service to those palefaces who still wish to traverse Harm City, I have gathered seven typical accounts of oppressed on privileged aggression to use as case studies for the purpose of privileged preparation as opposed to perforation.

April, 2016, Essex, Baltimore County, MD

Two innocent, unarmed, oppressed individuals approached an older privileged oppressor and demanded reparations. The word used to get the privileged person's attention was, "Hey," followed by, "You got something for me?" The larger and silent of the two oppressed individuals got the older privileged person's arms and pinned them to his sides. In the meantime, the reparations recovery agent effected the recovery of the debt, at least in part. The privileged person was unharmed.

To prevent this from happening to you, you should never stop when somebody speaks to you. As you continue to move, if the aggressors continue to approach, move to one side or the other, whatever you have to do to keep one of these people between you and the other. If you are not confident in your ability to level both of these aggressors, do not move towards blocking terrain such as a wall or a hedge but into an open area, toward traffic, into the street if necessary. Running away, unless you are an adolescent boy or man in his twenties is usually not an option, and an unsuccessful effort to flee will leave you weakened and easily handled. You should have something on your person that you can grab as a weapon, even if it's just an umbrella, keys, flashlight, pen or pencil that you should hold as you continue to walk away from the aggressors.

If these people have approached you or made a verbal communication, then keep your eyes on them, even if it means walking backwards. If, however, they have not diverted in your direction and have not made verbal contact or threats about people looking like you, do not turn your head and look at them, as this could cause you to seem fearful and be targeted. The best thing you could do to keep an eye on them and not draw attention is to cross the street or in the case of being on a parking lot, walk away in a direction perpendicular to their line of travel, and at this time, look over your shoulder. It is common for people, even careless people and jaywalkers, to cross the street to turn their head and look for traffic in both directions. This is your cover for taking a look around. There are other methods for keeping an eye on people who may be following you, but in this case we are focusing on people with aggressive approaches.

Comments

» Add a comment «
Dave   May 1, 2016 8:52 AM EDT

"Reparations recovery agent." I'm totally stealing that one. I've really enjoyed this series and I can tell you enjoyed writing them. Appreciate the dry humor.

'Excuse me, Sir'
Black Spring Survival Guide #2

© 2016 James LaFond

April 2016, Parkville, Baltimore County

One man was walking to his car on a parking lot when two youths approached him. One of the youths said, "Excuse me, Sir," the other one had his hand in his pocket right before he reached his car where the two youths stood in front of the hood. The youth nearest the car and the line of cars in the parking lot had his right hand in his pocket; the other, larger youth, stepped up next to the man, effectively cornering him between the row of cars, his car and the youth. The boy with the gun blocked the lane between the man's car and the SUV parked next to him. The man was blocked by the front of the SUV to his left, and to his right, by the larger boy. As he considered turning and running and thought it was not an option, the larger boy said, "Give over your shit." The man handed over his wallet and his smart phone, and the boys fled.

Had the man turned and fled, if the boy was of a mind to shoot him, he would have made an excellent close target. Also, he could have been easily tackled by the larger boy if he had turned in front of him. This is typical of how hand guns are used in a robbery in the city with a technique modified in a parking lot, with the parked cars serving the function of the walls of a building in a city stick up. Once in this situation, the man was just in a horrible position.

There are three answers to this.

1. As soon as the boys are spotted, move to the left, through the lane of cars, as if your car is in another area and make your way back to the establishment you left to call the police.

2. Turn right and walk across the drive lane through the next row of cars, betting that the boy that was in line with you has the gun and the one advanced and to your right is the blocking partner in the case of a stick up and would now be between you and the possible shooter.

3. If things become apparent after you have passed the last gap in the cars to your left and the flanker is already to your right, if you are of a mind to fight, you should grapple with him and keep him between you and the other boy other boy as long as possible.

'Give it up, Lady'
Black Spring Survival Guide #3

© 2016 James LaFond

April, 2016, White Marsh, Baltimore County

A privileged woman was walking her dog after dark. The dog was a medium sized mutt. An oppressed young man approached, pulled out a knife, and demanded her money, saying, "Give it up, Lady." The lady backed away as the man approached, and the dog got between them. He slashed out with the knife and cut the lady, and then the dog bit him and he ran off.

For the female dog owners who could be in this situation, do not walk toy dogs. They will be the targets of larger, aggressive dogs and will not effectively protect you from men. In the case of a woman walking a medium sized dog, like this lady, always keep the dog between you and any man that approaches you by leaving the leash slack, giving the dog room to work and making the man have to walk around you. Encouraging the dog to bark is a good idea. Dogs of this size are pretty effective at warding off aggressors, because they're active, they're loud, and they can do some damage.

If you have a larger dog, do not make the mistake of choking up on the leash to protect the man that's approaching you to protect him from the dog. If you're close to the collar of your dog, grab the latch and tell the person who's approaching you, that you're about to let the dog off the leash. Suggested command, "Back off, or I'm letting him loose." Ideally, a woman walking a dog at night after dark should only have dogs of man-eating caliber: Rottweilers, Irish Wolfhounds, Dobermans, German and Belgian police dogs, and the Kuvasz. Also, urban people who aren't familiar with dog breeds will mistake a Greyhound for a Doberman. My favorite is the Rhodesian Ridgeback. These dogs are actually bred to dine on oppressed individuals of the melanin-rich variety. As with all street survival, avoiding or discouraging an aggressive approach is preferable to successfully defending. Usually, having a large dog is an effective deterrent.

'Could You Help Me Out With Some Directions?'
Black Spring Survival Guide #4

April, 2016, Middle River, Baltimore County

Last Monday night, out in Middle River, a lower class, middle aged white man was walking away from the bus stop when a younger black fella asked him for directions. When the man stopped to comply with the request, the young fella punched him out, and while he was on the sidewalk, took his backpack, which also contained his prescription medication.

This is the most common ruse in the world and is no different from someone asking you for the time or for a cigarette or change. These are generally attempts to test your complaisance and determine whether or not you will be attacked.

What to do if you are asked for directions, or the time, or a cigarette?

1. Play dumb. Literally behave as if you did not hear them. This only works well if you are moving past them or away. Develop the habit of never turning your head when addressed by someone you do not know. This does piss off cops, so be careful. If you are stuck in their space waiting for a bus for instance, then you

are essentially doing #2 below. This is why walking is safer than taking the bus.

2. Make eye contact and say nothing. Half of them will try to escalate into a fight right here, which is better than you getting sucker punched.

3. Keep moving or keep your distance by stepping away as you apologize for not having what they want.

Verbally engaging beyond these limits is not recommended and will generally result in a fight or ambush. Verbal engagement with blacks is almost always a bad idea, as 90% of them have been raised by bitch queens to argue with the police and use verbal escalation to build courage for an attack and/or cohesion for a mob attack.

If you do give directions do so while at a distance by talking loudly and pointing.

'Yo, Whachyo Doin' Wit My I-Phone?'

Black Spring Survival Guide #5

© 2016 James LaFond

April, 2016, Parkville, Baltimore County

A white boy was walking away from school at noon when he was approached by three classmates who were the oppressed victims of some more privileged white-boy. The boy was verbally intimidated and pushed around until he gave up his property. He identified the three thugs to the school police and they were arrested, to be released to exact revenge soon. Hopefully this boy's parents have removed him from school and sent him to live with other relatives.

What Can Boys Do To Prevent Muggings By Schoolmates

You must make your self into a skilled, conditioned, hyper-aggressive combatant and immediately attack any individual or group that insults or threatens you. You must be a badass, otherwise you're just ass.

This same thing happened to one of my fighters in Parkville when he was 16-years-old and he immediately punched the biggest bully [who was the captain of the Parkville Senior

High Wrestling Team] in the chest, splitting his sternum in half.

Another one of my fighters was the only white boy in an all black city school and was attacked by armed individuals and groups every day. He eventually got expelled for knocking out to many negroes.

Either way, once in a school that tolerates this, or is populated by blacks, you will have three choices:

1. Be beaten and robbed regularly

2. Drop out of school

3. Get expelled from school for martyring the hero children of the welfare state.

When I was in high school about three in ten black boys could fight and two in ten whites. Now, one in ten combatants is the most you see in any white or black mix. This is a pussy generation. Be an apex predator and break ribs and noses, and scatter teeth across the hallway until the limp-dicks and cunts that run these pig pens for inseminating young minds with their rancid complacency kick you out. In the mean time the white girls will suck your cock and the black girls will try to have your baby. Enjoy life while you are young, before you can get locked up for punching all of these wimps out.

Read Taboo You, join a boxing gym and a judo club and smack these punks down.

Oh yes, if you have a cute teacher, understand that her husband is a wimp and she needs to gat railed by a real man. So get her to slide her phone number into your back pocket while the school cop takes you away in handcuffs for knocking out Jerome and Tweezlebee.

'Give it Up, Yo'
Black Spring Survival Guide #6

© 2016 James LaFond

April, 2016, Middle River, Baltimore County

Out on the Redneck Waterfront, where I work, where real white men still walk the streets in defiance of Black Supremacy, Bill was walking home from work at about Ten on a weekday night, at the true end of the welfare month, when the welfare mammies send their young bucks out looking for white folks to rob. On the secondary street of Orems Road a car with two black dudes pulled up next to the sidewalk on which Bill was walking. The two guys bailed out and demand that Bill hand over his money. Never having worked for a living, or having known an employed person, these two idiots did not realize that it was Thursday night and Bill didn't have shit on him. But he fought anyway, fought the two bucks to stand a still, until another car with two more black thugs in it rolled up and joined the fight against their evil oppressor.

Unlikely to prevail against four guys at once, Bill stood his ground on the sidewalk and began yelling for help in this white residential area, unfortunately still inhabited by real white men who do not appreciate the government moving gangs of predators into nearby Essex to prey upon them. Soon porch lights came on, doors began opening, and the sissy Negroes fled the scene without Bill's paltry end-of-the-week cash.

What Should a Paleface do in Bill's Situation?

Do what Bill did!

I might suggest picking up garden bricks when a car rolls up and launching one through the windshield and maintaining the other to cave in a yammering coconut. The cops might come after you for the damage to the car but it will help prevent these sissies from driving off effectively when your neighbors get on the scene. This is a neighborhood invasion and should be treated like one.

Fuck the police!

'One in Ten'

American Street: Inside the Most Dangerous Neighborhood in America

© 2016 James LaFond

This is another Charle Laduff short on Detroit. This place looks like a post-apocalyptic ghost town, the kind of place that America was designed to be. I am serious about that, and do honestly think that old west gunfighters, marshals, mountain men and saloon keepers would be at home in such a place. I am enjoying my own congested version of the ghost town now, looking out my open window watching a cop cruise by the crackhouse three doors up looking for anything but what is there.

https://www.youtube.com/watch?v=yoyEu3MQqSk

Force Five from Bayonne
Reparation Recovery Training Needed for Rookie Agents, Says Black Spring Activator Justin W. R. Justice

© 2016 James LaFond

What is an activator?

Fool. You're plucking my last nerve.

An activator is an activist who is also serving as a reporter.

Any more stupid questions, Mantrovious?

Well, then get on up the way en get me one a dem Burger King bacon cheeseburgers for a dolla-thirty-nine.

Why not Mickey-Dees? Is you stupit—a-course you is, yo mutha were stupid when I tapped you into existence.

'Cause Mickey-Dee done gone traitorous on our shit and took away the dolla menu! Now git!

Now all I got ta do is figure out how this talk-type niggatech roll en I'll be crankin' out articles like that Harlin Munchkin back in da old ass day... Yeah, now this shit is rolling...

As Black Spring kicks into second gear I detect some gear grinding in the box. Apparently, y'all trifling fools didn't get the memo that this is about repayment for Whitey raping Great Grandmammy. So—en this just come to my attentive ears three weeks late, so the damage is unreparably done—when Black Spring Recovery agents are organized for an operation, they are supposed to target Whitey, supposed to pocket some cracker's shit, not go and take from your own, you dumbshits!

Look, it ain't like I'm getting paid for this joint. Malcolm ain't answering calls or returning texts and I haven't seen a dime to compensate for my time. So listen up, y'all, 'cause this is Justin W. R. Justice reporting on your dumbasses to try and salvage this shit!

Way back on April 14 the Tyronater—his fight name, 'cause he in training for that UFC—a brother with a job no less, was walking home down Belmar from training, when three bruthas and two sistas decide to bank his ass, talking shit about he got their cellphone.

The first mistake, is blacks can't pay reparations 'cause they owed them—unless a course it a fine bitch who Marry a white man en then you can take her shit 'cause it's jointly held under the law and she a traitor bitch anyhow. Besides that, they are not the enemy,

115

the oppressor of our situation, Whitey and his little Korean en Haji buddies, are the enemy.

The second mistake was, is you fools picked on a nigga who can thrown down. So what does that stupidness get you? The three of you made to look like sissiy faggots holding your nose while Yolanda trying to raise her big brother on the phone to come straighten this obstinate nigga out, only we know that Yolanda's big brother be bangin' Charniqua's aunt up in Charniqua's mamma's apartment, so that shit ain't goin' nowhere. And what is worse, by the time the Tyronater gets done with you bitch-ass niggas Charniqua just about ready ta have his baby!

You young fools need ta get your shit right. You should have used Charniqua—en even that scary bitch Yolanda—to put the seduction suction on his ass and recruit him to knock around the occasional hard-headed whiteboy that might throw a Yeti wrench into the entire Reparations Recovery effort.

This is Justin W.R. Justice straightening shit out up in here. Let's get on track, people.

Righteous Redistribution

Hunting Privileged Breeders Might Be The Way to Redeem Your Race, Says Justin W. R. Justice

© 2016 James LaFond

I am happy to report, my brothers and sisters, that the final week of the Sacred Month of Uprising was righteously celebrated with dozens of Reparations Recovery Teams working hard across Northeast Baltimore and Baltimore County. The Middle River Boys deserve the most credit, because they are bringing it into Polar Bar territory. For every brother out in Middle River there are 8 white boys, but we are still ruling the streets.

A sound strategy for Reparations Recovery Agents is to go after white bitches with their babies.

First, there are not many of them, so they are easy to spot.

Second, white crackers all seem to think the police are going to protect their bitches, witch ain't happening.

Third unlike our bitches, white bitches can't fight!

Most importantly, unlike our bitches, white bitches care about their children getting hurt and killed.

So let this be a lesson to you:

On Tuesday, April 26, on the very anniversary of the Sacred Uprising, this dumb white bitch was walking home with her purse in one hand and her little cracker baby in the other hand. Now a black bitch would have made that child walk. But no, this bitch is all defenseless and what not, as if some white men might defend her when they could be watching porn and playing video games.

Lo and take hold, as the clock said 10:50, three brothers jumped out of the bushes that surround the apartment complex where they live. One of the Reparations Recovery Agents grabbed her purse for impound and she tried to hold on to it. To which these three hardened brother, recently moved out of the city said, "Bitch, we will whoop yo ass and beat yo baby too!"

The white bitch came to her senses and let go of her purse, which contained all her money, which I trust was donated to The Cause.

Do not steal, reparate and keep it real—Justin W.R. Justice reporting.

A Crooked Smile of Relief
Under the Lie in Baltimore

© 2016 James LaFond

Yesterday I stopped at the ghetto food store to pick up some deals and it was packed with subsidized oppressed individuals getting their checks cashed—checks issued to drug addicts by a city program. Two of these black men were threatening white employees, and another was threatening a white drug addict for being alive, as they waited for their turn at the window.

All I found to purchase was heavy whipping cream for 2 pints per dollar, an excellent price, if I can figure out what to use it for—Ramen Stroganoff perhaps?

As I left, a girl that once worked for me, who saw me chase thugs off the parking lot of another store years ago, was standing outside grimacing, waiting for her cab to show up as she looked warily at two young thugs who were loitering and smoking, scouting for victims, for easy marks. She said "Hello, James."

I asked her how things had been at work.

She said, "Well, it's been almost two years since it was safe to take the bus, and all these news motherfuckers talk about is Freddie Gray and Black Lives Matter and we're [working whites in Hamilton] getting our asses kicked. Theses news people won't let it go, like they want another riot. The girls and I were talking about how it's going to go this year. If the first couple people they hit don't fight back it'll be on, they''ll be jumping on us as soon as

121

we hit the pavement. I hope they come after you."

"Oh, come-on, Kelly, I know I was a prick but I don't deserve that."

"Prick! You were a fucking asshole. But you fucking have balls, not like that security guard hiding inside from these guys."

"What, you mean these two faggots?" I said, as I pointed to the two innocent, unarmed, oppressed youth harmlessly assessing everyone that came and went.

"Oh, there's more, a lot more. They're multiplying—a couple of real men and they'd be gone."

"I don't do public services and the Guardian Angels have been barred from patrolling by the City and the County. If they lay a hand on me, I do promise to disembowel them. I always carry a knife now."

She gave me a crooked sigh of relief as the two thugs walked off [they had not heard us], going their separate ways with whatever intelligence they had gathered, and said, "Thanks a lot, Lonny Tune. You drop Mammas Little Boy anywhere near here and they burn Hamilton to the ground. What a world. Later, space invader."

Reparating Three Deep
Justin W. R. Justice Insituating on the Hunt for Whitey

© 2016 James LaFond

During the observances of the first anniversary of the Sacred Uprising, our Reparations Recover Agents were working hard divesting Whitey of that privilege. First out in Essex, where white people should not be allowed to walk untaxed, it has finally come to pass that not a white bitch or a white faggot-bitch is safe on the street because we rolling three and four deep, My bruthas!

Adreonaryus, Lentaveone and Begrillenit spotted this white faggot walking near the apartments down across from Middlesex Shopping center, as if his cracker ass should even be allowed out after dark. Knowing that the poleese were not going to do shit, and that the other crackers would just blame this fool for being out at night when faggot-white-bitches is supposed to be playing they video games, they just grabbed his ass and Lentaveone said, "Bitch, give it the fuck up!"

And don't your black-asses know that this white fagot handed over his cellphone—not even a smart phone this bitch was so pathetic—and his money.

You young Reparators take heed:

1. Find you a white taxpayer who is doubly a bitch, working for The Man—that's right, capitalize all that shit—THE MAN, and paying off the government and is therefore a natural bitch used to being banked.

2. Hunt in areas frequented by poor white folks, because the only things cops worry about in those areas is busting these sorry white bitches for smoking they weed and popping they pills.

3. The beautiful thing is, not only won't the poleese look for you, they will search him, run a check on his ass—which will take longer if you took his I.D. and might even get his bitch-ass locked up—and they will give him shit for walking in your hood at night. Brutha, you own the night!

4. Last, and definitely not least, is that where you and your boys would pack up to avenge this kind of shit, white faggots don't play that. This bitch-ass white-nigga will have no big brutha to come hunting your ass, no daddy with a gun, no little brutha scouting you for a payback. No, once this bitch-ass white-nigga is done, he done!

This is Justin W.R. Justice, reminding real bruthas and sistas to go hunt some sissy white folks.

2 Beats the Hell Out of 1

Justin W. R. Justice Exporting the Fo Real Tax Initiative, with an Interview of T. Spoone "the self-hating coon" Slickens

© 2016 James LaFond

Brutha, you know how hard-headed a black man gets when somebody come up in his home?

Shit, most bruthas will even fight the poleese up in their crib rather then be seen looking like a bitch going down easy in front of their baby's mamma and the little shits she's had with otha niggas—so he will fight.

White folks, on the other hand, generally freeze when the poleese and other such— unless he one of those suicidal types who will fight, who just shot his wife—aggressors come up in they house. Now, though I don't much care for what this Old-Ass Coon has to say about black folks, I did consult Urban Scholar, T. Spoone Slickens as to why Whitey is typically so paralyzed when people kick in his front door, and this is what that self-hating coon had to say:

"Understand, that as we evolved to be loud and rambonoxious out on the savannas with lions and other bigass rampaging shit trying to stomp us back up into the trees from which we fell, so did white folks evolve, but under less favorable conditions. Now white folks evolved from Neanderthaws, and their fear from way back in these caveman days is vested in the story of The Three Little Nigs and the Big Bad Landlord, which is right on topic here, so it's a shame really, that it has not been made into a movie. So here it goes.

"You got three little broke-ass nigs—and this is how white folks do, throw their fairytale anxiety upon lesser races—who owed they rent to this big bad landlord who done looked like Battista [https://en.wikipedia.org/wiki/Dave_Bautista] leaping right off the WWE TV set into their broke-ass shit. The three little nigs know he's coming to collect the rent, for which reason he had left the doors off of the apartments he rented them, so he wouldn't have to break his own shit down when rent came due.

"Now the first broke-ass nig was a heroin junky, who tried masking-taping newspapers to his front door, and don't you know the landlord just walked right through that trifling attempt at tenant contempt!

"Next door down, that crack-head nig, he up and duct-taped cardboard, and even reinforced that mess with baling wire and milk crates—but the big-ass buff landlord was not having that shit and come crashing in roaring, 'Where's my rent!'

"But the tweaker nig down the hall, that ever-busy asphalt jungle bunny done ripped all of

128

the bricks out of the loft wall that faced the street, bricked the apartment doorway up, and while that big Battista-looking somebody tried to bust his way through the bricked up doorway, climbed out the ruined street wall and actually stole the landlords car!

"Okay, I know that is a lot to absolve, but what it basically comes down to, is that us colored folks are loud and fast to deal with lions, and white folks are quiet and conniving—you see, the tweaker in the story represented the white man—from living in caves that might fall in if they got loud and might be invaded by some big-ass brown bear. So, when some African American home invader comes through the door, that Neanderthaw 'Oh, shit, I'm bear food, play dead so he'll eat my wife while I crawl away back into the deep part" gene kicks in, and if he has not had time to upgrade his cave entrance, he's pretty much left with playing possum until that shit blows over. This cave bear thing, might I remind you, also explains white racism—cause we big and brown and they still scared-ass cavemen inside."

Thank you, Mister Slickens for cooning us in on that.

So, bruthas and sisters, on the last day of the Scared Week of Uprising, two bruthas saw this bitch-ass white nigga crossing the parking lot of the El Rich motel, out in White Marsh, where he had been tapping some of that lovely latina pussy, and attempted to run his ass down, figuring he would not have the legs to get away—but don't you know that scared-ass white-boy must a been on crack becaue he outran their asses and made it into his motel room.

And in they came, shoulder first, demonstrating that Reparations Recovery Agents shall not be stopped in their righteous quest for redistribution. The bitch was hiding in the bathroom, so they left her be but did take her cell phone along with his and all of his ill-gotten white gain.

This is Justin W. R. Justice, announcing that I'm going on the road, exporting recovery efforts wherever they need importing.

Keep it real, and don't forget, you are Reparating, for from Whitey, it is impossible to steal.

T. Spoone Slickens, Inquire

The Truth About Black Folks

Dust Cover

T. Spoone Slickens, Inquire, was born during a tropical storm on Cape Fear, North Carolina. He has recently emerged as a scholar of the urban American experience, teaching from his janitorial closet in the basement of a dying catholic church in Baltimore City.

This volume includes his essays:

The Cure for What Ails Whitey

Miechlin Mikya's Free Lunch

'Smart White Folks?'

Scrimp Boy Sam's Bouquet

Donell Weston's Bitchegg Hotel

Also features the secret interview with Stefan Molyneux **The Truth about Black America**.

"Game recognizes game—and game recognizes the shit out of no game."

-Wallace

For Ajay and Erika, two of my
favorite people

The Cure for What Ails Whitey

Literal Face Saving Advice for Sufferers of Stupid White People Syndrome Stuck In An African American Ethical Zone

© 2015 T. Spoone Slickens

In describing the ethical nuances of the urban black American psyche I have elected to lean on a learned soul, who is a black man himself, and is better able to illuminate the gentrification conundrum that Whitey—and his high and mighty wife—finds himself in.

I give you, T. Spoone Slickens, Inquire, foremost authority on the Black Urban Experience in America.

"Class, what is the definition of the African American Ethical Zone?"

"Bitches, is you stupit!?!"

"Just look at the picture of the burning police van that that smartass whiteboy made a icon of for this informatory joint up in here!"

"Class dismissed."

"Are you sassin' me boy?"

"Look Mister I-wanna-be-a-smart-nigga-when-I-grow-some-hair-on-these-balls, Lesson One—and that shit is capitalized—has done been taught. Now git!"

Stupid White People Syndrome, by
T. Spoone Slickens, Inquire

Why do we Black folks need to find a cure for white stupidity?

That is pretty simple to answer by way of a question that this brain dead generation can fathom.

That question is, where is Denzel?

Exactly! If life were a Denzel Washington movie things would be alright for white folks, because they would have Black Superman there to sort things out. For this reason it is of the utmost importance to define Stupid White People Syndrome and offer a course of self-treatment for these folks. This is important, because, while they may be delusional, they have also invented almost everything your greedy little paws touch upon. If we just let these people self-destruct we'll be back to living in huts a month after that last EBT card swipes for insufficient funds.

SWPS is an affliction of white folks who believe in a single standard of behavior for all of humanity. Not only do they believe that this single standard should exist, but that it does exist! Unbeknownst to these dumbasses is an entire world of seven-point-a-lot-a-billion colored folks who basically don't believe in the useless shit white folks believe in. Now, that is okay when some hairy ass head hunter in East Bumfuck Mucluc don't believe in passing up an easy kill. So long as that dumbass white person stays out of East Bumfuck Mucluc.

However, what you have in these here Disunited States of West Judea, is a bunch of dumbass hard-headed black folks crowded together—and wanting to spread out—while at the very same Newsblessed time, a bunch of dumbass soft-headed white folks with money want to sip coffee that's been grown without some dumbass Latino peasant getting his ass whooped for being too slow about the process, in the very same shithole recently vacated by starving crack whores chasing those Wal-Mart Pop Tarts out into White Man's Land — renovated, of course.

Obviously, as a former white man of repute once said, to some knuckleheaded white man wearing striped pants, "What we have here, is a failure to communicate."

This white accredited course is in three segments. Each is an actual incident which occurred in Baltimore, Maryland, in the second week of May, in the year of our disappointed Lord two-thousand and fifteen. These will be posted separately on this crazy white man's website, so that you sidewalk crawlers can access it on your mamma's Obama phone. These lessons, or study segments as the contemporary jargon goes, shall consist of—and shall be read by your impatient asses in the proper order so as not to confuse that Jello that's trying to take on a mold between your ears:

1. Miechlin Mikya's Free Lunch

2. Scrimp Boy Sam's Bouquet

3. Donell Weston's Bitchegg Hotel

Until then, I am T. Spoone Slickens, your educator.

Miechlin Mikya's Free Lunch

White Wednesday Guest Author, T. Spoone Slickens on Stupid White People Syndrome

© 2015 T. Spoone Slickens

Miechlin Mikya is a young black woman who is built like that white cartoon man who advertises tires. Therefore her street name is Miechlin, after the company that sells those tires. That might seem cruel to white folks— where it is merely an accurate state of critical observance to us black folks. What is cruel, is the second name in her street name, which is the first portion of her three part government name: Mikya, really? What was her crack ho mother smoking that decided her on naming her only ghetto-begotten daughter after the sound made by an Eskimo slurping down whale blubber?

This is not just an example of T. Spoone Slickens, Inquire, picking on another dumb ghetto fool. No, indeed. You see, when you young hoppers, who have done nothing and have accomplished even less, reproduce quite by accident, you get the bright idea of naming your baby hopper in such a way as to be not only meaningless, but nigh unpronounceable to white folks. This has two effects:

1. Some white folks will get angry about being forced to pronounce a stupid made-up ghetto name, and limit their discourse with you, which was of course your dumbass mother's idea, who thought no further ahead than pissing off the judge that would be hearing your case. White folks irritated by being harangued by you for misspelling something that is not spelled the way it is pronounced, or for pronouncing it like it is spelled, will limit their interactions with you. And since these very white folks have access to the opportunity that your dumbass

parents are always whining about not having access to, their declining to interact with you— or in cases where the law says they have to interact with you, minimizing said interaction— will limit your access to opportunity.

2. White folks who suffer from SWPS will feel sorry for your unlucky ass and will give you that which you should work for, thereby depriving you of crucial life lessons and opportunity for character development.

Now, despite her unfortunate twin moniker, Miechlin Mikya [who expects people who can read to pronounce the name on her name tag Mik-i-ya] has landed a job. She works as a cashier at one of the few retailers in the Mondawmin area that was not destroyed during the riots, where a small army of hood-rats destroyed the businesses and homes that made living in that wretched neighborhood bearable for black folks. There ain't a white person who buys squat up in there. White people see that [black people burning their own community], and think that all black people are stupid, causing them to forget their own raging stupidity, resulting in continued white stupidity.

Example: Mikya's Free Lunch

One day, as I was purchasing my Kenyan coffee beans at the grocer, Mikya was running Register #11, which I suppose is some kind of joke, beings how she cannot count that high, unless she breaks out those painted toenails, which she cannot see in any case.

There were three of us in line: a black lady, a white lady, and yours truly. While halfway through the black lady's appreciable order, Mikya, said, "I'm hungry—and this chicken looks good. I'll be right back."

To the white lady's astonishment, Mikya walked across the store to the fried chicken counter, placed an order, had the order filled, returned to her register, and then resumed ringing out that lady's order as she slurped on her unpaid for fried chicken!

The white lady then turned to me and said, "I can't believe this. How come the customer is not upset, has not called the manager—I'll call the manger and get this straightened out."

I shushed the lady and promised to enlighten her out of earshot of Mikya, who was casting eyes of intimidation about.

Mikya then rang out the black lady and took care of the white lady, before seeing to my payment, all the while sucking the chicken grease and breading from her painted nails. I walked the lady outside and informed her, as politely as I might, that she suffered from SWPS.

"Miss, the customer has been desensitized to rudeness, not in the manner of passive acceptance to rudeness, but as a matter of survival. For example, last year, a white man and woman on the bus with their handicapped child, refused to move out of the handicapped section to make way for a pack of hoodlum students. The bus driver—a black female—got on her phone and called her sons, and daughters and other younger relatives and had them waiting at the bus stop that she knew these white people got off at. When the white people got off at the stop they were promptly attacked by no less than eight youths."

"But that is not right!" she exclaimed.

"Indeed not, Miss. But consider, that the MTA driver makes upwards of thirty thousand dollars per year and has full benefits. Consider now Mikya, who makes ten thousand at most, and think, 'Would she not risk her relative pittance to maintain her status of queen in her own personal space, unassailable by ethics, morals, or other needling notions of right and wrong?'

"Miss, wrong indeed it is. But it is, and remains the reality, which your sense of right and wrong may not alter. To Mikya and the other ill-begotten progeny of a drug-addicted generation, right and wrong are merely fantastical notions that render those who ascribe to these fantasies vulnerable for exploitation. So, as you can see, the lady in line before you was in fact dealing effectively with the reality. Even if Mikya did not phone in a parking lot beating, the argument with her and the manager would have surely extended her stay beyond the time she was willing to remain."

"But, Sir," the well-dressed white lady said, "I would do the right thing, take time from my day to make certain that other customers were not so treated, and would demand that the store manager protect me on the way to the car."

At this point I had had too much, and looked her square in the eyes, raising my voice to an authoritative tone, "Miss, the entire Baltimore City Police Department was unable to safely make it to and from their vehicles in this very neighborhood a mere two weeks ago. Not a single one of the violent actors remains in custody or faces charges. What makes you think that white man in the white shirt and black tie is going to be able to protect you?"

The woman then became wistful and melancholy and said, "Thank you, but I have no desire to continue this conversation. I have become depressed and would speak of positive things or nothing. Goodbye."

And there you have it, embodied in one upscale white woman, a case of Stupid White People

Syndrome so far advanced as to resist all scholarly and persuasive attempts to remove it from the Caucasian brain, as if the very brain of the white person, so suited for innovation, has developed in such a way as to make the eradication of outdated ethical constructs difficult, if not impossible.

"Yes, Mi'Shaka, you actually have a lucid question? Presumably your FaceBook hos are being debased elsewhere in the nethersphere?"

[Expansive ebonic dialogue, redacted]

"So, Mi'Shaka, to paraphrase: now that you are convinced that Whitey is soft and guilt ridden enough to be displaced, you would emulate your savage namesake by importing white slave advisors to assure the smooth operation of your air conditioning unit and the video game console?"

[Affirmative obscenity-laced ebonic response, redacted]

"Yes, Mi'Shaka, it is commendable that you would emulate Shaka Zulu and General Toussaint, and opt not to eradicate the whites in light of their many uses. I could answer this now. But seeing as how I might use a lesson on white exploitation to lure you back into class participation for a record two times in one year, you will have to return tomorrow for your answer.

"Class, tomorrow, we will delve into a special study unit, courtesy of our aspiring post-apocalyptic warlord, titled, Smart White Folks: Who, How, When & Where."

'Smart White Folks?'

Who, How, When & Where, and How to Get You Some More, by T. Spoone Slickens, Inquire

"No Mai'K'law, the title following my name is not inquirer, which would merely be a tiresome busybody, but Inquire, or one who personifies the spirit of inquiry."

"In regards to Mi'Shaka's suggestion that an oppressed hoodlum, such as himself, might rise all high and mighty above the heights aspired to and conspired from by the likes of George I-Got-

Me-An-Ivy-League-A-Because-My-Daddy's-White-With-A-Capital-W Bush, by enslaving himself some of the smartest white folks to fall from the Ivy Tower-clinging vine of rarified society, I have prepared the following course for your dubious enlightenment.

"I know it ain't White Wednesday, Tuaca Tuesday. But I, T. Spoone Slickens, promised you young hoppers an extension of yesterday's lesson, and, as a negro of my word, I'll have your young ass know that it's so!"

Monitor, Monitor, on the Wall, Who Is The Smartest Ass of Them All?

Marilyn vos Savant, who is the wife of Robert Jarvik, M.D., inventor of the Jarvik 7 artificial heart, has a 228 point IQ!

Factored by pure wattage Marilyn is smarter than the entire Baltimore Ravens defensive squad. And, when you take into account that every black man who you add to a group, draws down the IQ of all black men in that group by

5.8 percentages—and that this shit geometrifies explorentially—then their asses will never beat her in a game of chess no matter how long they sit with their chins on their fists.

And no, Mi'Shaka, she did not have a bunch of mixed race babies so that you can collect them in your vinyl upholstered seraglio. This points up the problem with reproducing smart folks, namely that they have so much going on between their ears they do not spend the long hours of the night fornicating; which is what dumbass poor people do.

Therefore, we have a dearth of smart folks and a glut of stupit folks.

How Did White Folks Get So Smart?

So how did white people get so smart?

Permit me to condense the scholarly works of W. D. Fard—the many volumes of which would tax your bobbling brains into oblivion—into a succinct history of the origins of the white race.

The black scientists of Egypt, who had erected the pyramids and carved the Sphinx as beacons for the mother ships upon their return, wished to colonize the frigid zones of the earth.

Enter Big-Headed Yakub, a massive-brained man of great intellect. Ole Big Head decided to breed a race of slaves to colonize the misty reaches of Europe and drive the slant-eyed races into the Pacific—I digress, but this is where you got American Indians. The black scientists decreed that the Chinese and other such races could have the Western hemisphere, and encouraged them to migrate in advance of the hordes of ravening white cavemen—bred in great towering vaults in the catacombs of the island of Patmos in the year 5,700 before the Ascension of W. D. Fard, around about 1935.

There was a problem though, with the white slave race—Yakub put his very own brain juice up in those cracker heads! Not only that, but the whites were cross-bred with albino Chinamen and took on that anthill Asian work ethic!

"Now, how is your black ass gonna stop that stuff from blowing back on us?" said, the High Priest Yakuboda, to Big-Headed Yakub.

And don't you know, Yakub snatched the keys to the last mother ship from the peg below the time clock, and left Yakuboda and the other blacks high and dry—sound familiar to you?

So, let that be a lesson to you hoppers, that the same story that saw the creation of the white man saw the betrayal of the black man by his own—and here our sorry asses are!

When Have People Been Smartest?

This section and the next are indebted to Clifford A. Pickover, a man who God did not overlook when he was neglecting to hand out brains below the Alps—and the Mason Dixon Line.

Basically we are talking about Main-Entry Laws and their distribution. Main Entry Laws are at the basis of all your earthly gadgetry from can openers, to condoms to space stations.

Their historical distribution is like so:

250 B.C.-1700 A.D.... 20% [10 laws]

1700-1800 .... 12% [6 laws]

1800-1900................... 60% [30 laws—obviously had us some smart white people fucking back in this time]

1900-2000...................8% [with but 4 laws—and built on the others at that—what we have here is obviously, a failure of smart white people to copulate! Tesla, for instance, was brilliant—and had not a child, not even a woman with whom to make an attempt!

Where Were the Smartest White People Born?

Nation————-Main-Entry Laws

Germany..........14*

France..............12

Britain...............10

Ireland..............2

Netherlands.....2

Italy.................1 [that must be a typo!]

Switzerland......1 [clocks]

United States...1 [football]

Hungary..........1 [the bra]

Greece.............1 [Archimedes, smartest man in human history, butchered on his front lawn by another white man while he was figuring out how to talk to God with numbers.]

*Dropped more bombs on this joint than any place on earth this side of Vietnam—God only knows how much genius sperm got firebombed in that mess.

White Soul Driver End Time Action Plan

If any black man finds himself in possession of a post apocalyptic nation—or even a city block—I say to him, do not put on hockey masks and run at each other in armored dune buggies fighting over the last bit of oil, but find yourself some smart white men, and match them up with some

155

blonde haired white women—just to make sure there ain't no negro genes up in there—and get their narrow asses to breeding! It worked out just fine for Noah. You could build yourself an Ark too, stocked two-by-two with the smartest white people, so when God throws a comet this way we might be able to do more than pray.

Scrimp Boy Sam's Bouquet

White Hero Wednesday: An Exemplar of Smart Narrow-Assed White Virtue Enters the African American Ethical Zone at Great Peril

© 2015 T. Spoone Slickens

As a scholar of the African American experience, I, T. Spoone Slickens, your educator, have spent many an hour researching shopping patterns. These include those shifty tricks that Whitey plays on the black community, like putting the word 'Sunny' on a plastic bottle of yellow-tinted sugar water and placing it in the orange juice case. With the Hebrew influence in the grocery business such shenanigans are to be expected.

I have taken some heat for this last statement. However, as a life-long grocer in Central Maryland, I can tell you that I was trained by Jews and men who were trained by Jews, and that the largest grocery operation in the Mid Atlantic Region was run by an outstanding example of Hebrew kind for near fifty years. Also, three secondary food store chains have been operated by the Sons of Moses, where only two were run by Italians—one to fail miserably, the other dying as I write. And, but two Baltimore area market chains were run by blacks, both now defunct. Say what you will about The Slickens, but he is no anti-Jewite. Indeed, my current scholarly activations are being underwritten by my employer, a newsstand owner who operates the adjacent jewelry store.

As well, the diligent scholar should expect the hard-headed members of the poorly excavated black community to institute their own five-fingered 'reparations' initiative. Although the best these fools can hope for is to not get caught and cause the prices in the local market to rise.

Right in White Time

Shoplifting has ever been the bane of retail food managers. Baltimore, with its high level of addictions and entitlement, is a Mecca of petty thieves. They have traditionally come in four varieties:

1. The sneaks, who crumble when caught and go meekly

2. The runners—often crack heads—who make you chase them.

3. The fighters, the rare indignant shoplifter that insists he brought 73 boxes of Dove soap up into your store, and somehow still had a need to visit the soap section.

4. The freaks—often diseased—who will piss at you, squirt breast milk at you, and brandish syringes.

Beginning this spring, just before the riots—at the same time African cabbies were being stiffed for fares by threatening black men—a fifth kind of shoplifter has appeared: the Black Reparations Patriot! Rather than snagging this, that and the other over-priced thing on the down low, this knucklehead declares himself entitled to the unpaid for goods and marches right past—or even over—the manger or security guard, in the latter case, usually a black man himself.

Below are two examples from the second week of April, immediately following the Baltimore Riots of 2015.

Nutrina—I kid you not brother, that dumb ho mamma named her after a giant aquatic rat from South Bumfuck Brazil—was demanding a refund for an unsavory food item she claimed to have consumed, and for which she could not present a receipt.

Mister Fields, the sissy white man who manages that store, told this big girl flat out that she was not getting a refund. And, oh my, entirely against type, she laid his narrow ass flat out, like Queen Latifa whooping Gary Coleman!

Enter Scrimp Boy Sam, a fat slovenly example of Negro indigence, who enters the same store every day at about 3 p.m., and heads directly to the salad bar—which, in Maryland, often serves steamed shrimp spiced in the shell with Old Bay seasoning. Scrimp Boy Sam will take a handful of large "scrimps," meander on back to the men's room—filthy by any standard applied to the human dinner table—stands at the urinal and urinates, with no hands to control his errant sprinkler system as those are ever busy peeling and eating "scrimps." He leaves the shells in the urinal to boot.

That was a dumb black man's version of a petty crime. Now let us observe this same dumb black man's version of slavery reparations.

Scrimp Boy Sam, having eaten his fill of his mispronounced delicacy, decided that some lucky lady was in need of a bouquet of flowers—roses—and sauntered over to the front end from the flower department, past the registers, and proudly toward the front door, where little narrow-assed Shane, Assistant Whiteman on Duty—kind of like their narrow-assed version of an *HNC—blocked his way.

Sam, over six foot and easily 300 pounds, stopped, before actually stepping upon Shane, and said, "Lille white man, you need to ged outta ma way."

Our white hero then stood defiantly and declared, "You are not leaving with those flowers."

Sam retorted, "I'm takin' these flowers en you ain't stoppin' me, lille white man!"

Shane repeated that he would not permit the flowers to be removed from the premises without payment—not on his watch.

If I might digress, it is cute to the point of endearing how white folks will hold unto a long-tattered principal in the face of overwhelming odds.

Momentarily seeming to take pity on the little white assistant manager, Scrimp Boy Sam hesitated before walking over the man who was less than half his size, and in that instant of indecision lost the battle of wills, which Sly Little Whitey suddenly turned into a battle of wits—which is how they do—by reaching out and breaking the flowers in half, and saying, "Okay, now you can have the flowers."

Technically speaking, this encounter was a draw, with the little white man's brains making up for his lack of brawn. As pathetic a story as it is, the lesson should not be lost, that the black underclass no longer fears the police. As this trend continues expect Urban Reparations Patriots and the retailers they brazenly loot to up their game. Before this hardheaded year is out there will be a pitched battle somewhere, between a soft-headed white person who suffers from SWPS, and his staff, on one side, and the hardheaded black hoodlums that are now poised to overrun—in their own faux Napoleonic way—any shopkeeper who might defy them.

* HNC is an acronym meaning Head Negro in Charge.

"Mi'Shaka—watchyoudoin' sleepin' in my class!"

"Oh, so you thought Scrimp Boy was too stupid and Shane was too weak fo your rarified time!"

"Nigga, that was the entire point of the erection!"

"So now you wanna make amendments? I gotchyou hot-shot—Mister Walking Dead and runnin' that shit. You wanna A on this semester, you need to do your extra credit. Moses, pass the extra credit on back to...there you go, son."

"What Mi'Shaka?"

"Why, that would be your teacher's address."

"Well, you gonna cut the grass—a course!"

"Your mutha? Yo mutha gonna have some shit ta say 'bout this?"

"What, she about thirty?"

"Twenty-seven? All the betta... Bring her along en we can disgust your ass up in the air conditioning while you earnin' your extra credit in the yard."

"Class dismissed early y'all—Mista Slickens gotz some extra credit fo hisself today."

This unit will conclude with Donnell Weston's Bitchegg Hotel. And, in the meantime, do not forget to tune on for the T. Spoone Slickens Interview with Stefan Molyneux, which should air in the second week of August, in this year of our Disappointed Lord, 2015.

Donell Weston's Bitchegg Hotel

A Case Study in African American Economics: A Noted Black Scholar's Continued Effort to Educate White People

© 2015 T. Spoone Slickens

An essay, submitted to, and rejected by, The Cato Institute, by T. Spoone Slickens, Inquire.

This past May, in the wake of the hood-rat uprisings that glazed the eyes of Sissy America with fear and womanly longing for a protector, I found myself at wits end. At sixty years I'm stretched a might thin.

There is the newsstand job working for Mister Goldman.

Then there is the janitorial work at the church, and my education of the young ones, who skip class at the phony government school and come to me for a real education in the unused church gymnasium.

And then there are the women pining for a real man, all of a sudden wondering what they will do when the ghetto belches forth its pitiless progeny once again.

Mrs. Schaffer is an example of one such concerned citizen of the motherly kind, who came to the janitorial closet after mass and asked me to accompany her up the side street, back into the neighborhood where she lives, behind the church. She was a big old white queen, half-dyke by the look of her beat-down husband, so I knew this was not going to be another, 'Please Mister Slickens, walk me home, for I am afraid of those other negroes,' request for protection.

Oh no. Mrs. Schaffer was of a mind to discover the root cause of the urban blight that has engulfed her once middle-class street, lined with large frame houses that could each seemingly accommodate a boxcar load of Mexicans.

My reason for writing this paper are the same as my reason for accompanying Mrs. Schaffer up her street, to describe the activities she was witnessing with a bemused eye for what they truly where, the natural life cycle of the Government Subsidized Urban American Negro.

The Bitchegg Hotel and Environs

Some of these houses are boarded up.

Some are dilapidated and uncared for, the elderly residents unable to cut the lawn and trim the bushes.

Though provided with raised concrete sidewalks, no man walks the street in a neighborly way. There is only the coming and going of the busy man, remaining in the light of the friendless day or the crime-ridden night for only so long as is required to turn the key to his front door.

Some houses, such as the Schaffer residence, are models of suburban Americana nestled in the city.

Some of the houses are 'busted up' [this being the local terminology] into rentals, three apartments to a house, with a range of mostly single adult tenants.

Then there are the problems—three to be exact.

There is the unspecified business on the corner of the main street, which rents out the top floor to two bachelors, who patronize the local prostitutes. These prostitutes buy their drugs from boys selling dope at the gas station across the street.

There is the halfway house, whose occupants are all drug-addicted subjects of the Maryland

Corrections System, sentenced to live a period in this halfway house. This is a coed house, with men outnumbering women. The women prostitute themselves to the men for the money to buy drugs—you guessed it, white people—at the gas station. The residents are all temporary and tested weekly for drugs, which makes them *very* temporary. About half of these men patronize the drug dealers at the gas station. Of six men and two women residing here, both women and four of the men will return immediately to the drug-addicted life.

Servicing the dubious needs of the temporary residents of a troubled nature which the government has imported into this once viable neighborhood, are Donell Weston and the occupants of his bitchegg hotel.

Donell Weston is a slightly large man in his early thirties. He never puts hands on dope, but facilitates all dope distribution in this four block grid in Baltimore City. His work force consists of two men, four youths, and four children.

Donell and the men specialize in violent and intimidating solutions to the very foreseeable problems that beset his business model.

The four youths run drugs and collect money through a network of street dealers, who see each of these youths as the top of their little drug world, insulating Donell.

The four children are lookouts and messengers, and will one day rise to drug runner status.

Donell's house is called a hotel, because neither he nor the majority of the residents actually reside their on a consistent basis. The primary residence for each of the three men is the government-subsided apartment of their primary baby's mamma. There will be at least one secondary baby's mamma, in another government-subsidized apartment, to provide a hiding spot or refuge.

The primary residence of each of the four youths is their mamma's home, somewhere in the neighborhood. It is important for the exposed risk-takers among the crew to be residents of the neighborhood in which they deal. The reasons include knowledge of the area and a believable reason for being in the area. Most importantly, when arrested, these youth will be traced to their mamma's address and not associated with the hotel.

The four children [really 3-6 depending on occupancy patterns at the hotel] do reside at the hotel. These children are the children of crack whores, welfare whores and wino bitches, and are fathered by men not associated with Donell. His relationships with these women are limited to impregnating them, so that they may earn additional government EBT cash and food credit, and hopefully qualify for their own government-subsidized residence. Their older children by other men serve Donell as lookouts and messengers for small gifts of money. Typically, after one of these impregnated whores 'drops her bitchegg' she will apply for section eight residency elsewhere, and move on when possible.

This reptilian family structure must have a nexus. For one thing, Donell, a convicted felon with no children carrying his name, no taxable income, and no work record, is in no position to rent this property. For this reason, the primary resident, who is the Lady Lord of this bitchegg hotel, is the Queen Bitch Up in Here. Only Donell, who is her exclusive paramour—as a Queen Bitch, though rarely having any two children by the same man, she generally practices fidelity for the term of her rule over this residency—will address this woman by her name. The children, women and lesser males will tend to address her as Mamma. Mamma, alone, will receive any of Donell's significant cash income. She can get the house without him. She is the 'maker breaker' and he the 'money maker.' Together they become something of a mutated parody of man and wife.

Eventually, Donell may be killed or arrested. In which case, the hotel will devolve in upon itself as a stagnant nest of squalor, the boys raised therein taking up a life of crime, with Donell as their role model, and eventually, one day, possibly founding a bitchegg hotel of their own.

In the rare case that this crackhouse—which will have rooms for the halfway house people and other drug addicts to smoke their crack, shoot their dope and have their unseemly sex— is actually raided and shut down by the police, the Queen Bitch—arrested or not—will be unlikely to be able to maintain her residency and subsidized status at this location and will be forced to move on. This will effectively shut down the hotel, which will, gradually or abruptly, become vacant.

The business model behind the bitchegg hotel is simple: the criminal mates with a woman, who is married to the government, as he maintains a primary residence elsewhere. If said criminal is not astute, or if luck abandons him, as it often does in his chosen line of work, the bitchegg hotel may close within months. Normally, such arrangements endure for one to three years, with five years being the longest run I am aware of.

So there you have it, the African American Economy of Mrs. Schaffer's side street, explained by an examination of its nexus, Donell Weston's Bitchegg Hotel.

The Truth about Black America

With T. Spoone Slickens, Inquire: the Interview with Stefan Molyneux

© 2015 James LaFond, Transcribing for Mister Slickens

The following transcript is to a video recorded, but not aired, by Free Domain Radio, on 8/21/15.

"Hello, hello, everyone, this is Stefan Molyneux of Free Domain Radio, speaking. I trust you are doing well. Today we have a very special guest, T. Spoone Slickens, Inquire—his real name if you can believe that. Mister Slickens is with us from his home town of Baltimore, to discuss, the truth about Black America. Thank you so much, Mister Slickens, for taking the time today."

The Interview

Mister Slickens: "Thank you Mister Molay—it's an honor to be speaking with you."

Stefan: "Okay...ah, yes. We're looking into your home town, what with the recent riots—unrest, now, I think they call it. If we could begin with your education—you being an urban educator."

Mister Slickens: "I received my disinformation, or brain washing, from Gardenville Elementary School and then Hamilton Middle School. I then escaped the clutches of Leviathan, with my thankfully stubborn mind intact, at age fourteen."

Stefan: "So your 'higher' education was had where?"

Mister Slickens: "The Lexington Market, where I watched the debates between the Korean Christians, the Black Muslims, and the Black Jews. I would listen to these old fellows go at it about this, that and the other thing, and would then go up to the Enoch Pratt Library—the main branch—and do my fact checking. I subsequently found, that no matter how off a man was in his opinion, that something he said would spark a fruitful inquiry."

Stefan: [Suppresses a wide grin, unsuccessfully, turns his shoulder toward the camera, recovers, and interjects.] So, that is where you received the sobriquet 'Inquire?' Why not Inquirer?"

Mister Slickens: "That was already taken, nationally, and in Philadelphia."

Stefan: "So where did your inquiring mind take you—but first, to what do you attribute your stubborn refusal to be indoctrinated by the state schools and which drove you on your quest to learn."

Mister Slickens: "I was born during a tropical storm on Cape Fear, North Carolina, touched by reality in the womb if you will."

Stefan: [Suppresses broadening grin and nervously scratches back with right hand.] "So, with the inspiration of the harrowing circumstances of your birth, and having been transplanted to Baltimore—as part of the Great Migration, I assume—you went where for the continuation of your education, at the tender age of fourteen?"

Mister Slickens: "To the Arcade Newsstand at the corner of Hamilton and Harford Roads, between the hotdog joint, now a pizza joint, and the theatre, now a storefront church."

Stefan: "So, having dropped out of a Baltimore City middle school at the age of fourteen, and then having listened to religious fanatics argue theology at some market place, and visiting the library to—I am assuming—debunk their arguments, you went on to 'graduate school' if you will, to the newsstand."

Mister Slickens: "Yes, Sir. I was too young to sell the tobacco products, so could not run the register. I was tasked with stocking the literature, cleaning, and also reading as much as I could in order to engage in discussion and debate with the patrons, mostly older white men. My employer encouraged this, noticing that these men stayed longer, bought more coffee, and often purchased an extra copy of a magazine for me to take home and study up on. I was, you might say, the main intellectual attraction."

Stefan: "Was there any further education, other than your own reading, that has prepared you to take on your self-appointed role as an 'Urban Educator?'"

Mister Slickens: "Yes, Father Duncan, Pastor of Saint Dominick's, who frequented the newsstand, took me under his wing and taught me the finer points of the written word, including Latin. Once I got to reading those old Latin texts I came to understand, that all though the Romans were a sinful slave-driving bunch, they did not put stock in a man's race, only his behavior, his character, his value to society. This realization, that we Americans lived in a fantasy land of delusion, lit the spark in my brain to get to the bottom of this mess."

Stefan: "Who was your favorite Roman author?"

Mister Slickens: "Caesar. I've read the Conquest of Gaul a dozen times, at least."

Stefan: "Not Marcus Aurelius?"

Mister Slickens: "Once was enough there. How seriously can you take a man who produced such a murderous brat as Commodus?"

Stefan: "Excellent point—though favoring Caesar to such an extent is, should we say—p"

Mister Slickens: "Manly, it's a man's book, on being a man, conquering men, ruling men, and outsmarting the rest of the men."

Stefan: "Yes, peachy, paradise."

Mister Slickens: "Exactly."

Stefan: "Moving forward, despite your eschewing of formal education—which I can absolutely understand considering your choices—I'd like to explore the parenting aspect of life that you alluded to in regards to Marcus Aurelius and his maniac son."

Mister Slickens: "Certainly, Steven." [Stefan grimaces and tightens his fist.] It is my belief that the ancient practice of the slave masters in breaking up the family in order to maintain control, has been inherited by the State, and has been refocused on Black America with a vengeance. This assault on the Black family has been so successful that the evil eye of government has now been turned on whites and others. After all, it was a southern white man who started the welfare swindle. Speaking of which, by bringing in the Latino labor force to keep Native Born Americans in a vulnerable position, the State is now forced to ramp up its attack on the family, in order to crack the tough Catholic nut of the Hispanic working class. Those little folks don't know the State is coming for them, and likely won't notice until it has extinguished the family in the rest of America."

Stefan: [Stefan seems to be speaking to his assistants.] "That was actually quite good—perhaps original."

Stefan: "I understand you to be a teacher in some capacity?"

Mister Slickens: "Yes, indeed. For the past thirty years I have been the janitor at Saint Dominick's Church. Being as these white Catholics are dying off like flies or fleeing to the suburbs in droves, there is an under use of the facility. This has left me steward of considerable space in the basement of the church when it is not being used for those cry baby meetings of those whining drug addicts and alcoholics. Some of the local children who skip school, such as I had, have come to me for guidance. I usually have a class of two to five, with parental permission of course."

Stefan: "Mister Slickens, miraculously enough, you and I seem to be in absolute agreement that the removal of the father from the life of the child—particularly the son—is key to generating the outright savagery and brutality witnessed in your home town and in other American cities currently languishing under the withering eye of the State. Let us go to number two. What, in your opinion, is the key aspect of black parenting—as it stands—in generating such epidemic levels of crime and violence in the Black Community?"

Mister Slickens: "It's the violent black mother, whooping her son that has caused much of this."

Stefan: "You may not be aware of this, but I have done an entire series of videos and books on non-violent parenting. I can't agree with you enough that spanking—or as you call it whooping—is at the core of our social disfunction."

Mister Slickens: "Oh, a man whooping his son, or a woman spanking her daughter or small child, is no big thing. What is damaging is when you have a boy being emasculated before puberty even hits, by his big-ass mamma trying to be a man."

Stefan: "Whoa, whoa—are you seriously rationalizing the striking of children as an acceptable aspect of parenting?"

Mister Slickens: "I am."

Stefan: "Mister Slickens, were you spanked, or beaten as a child?

Mister Slickens: "I was never spanked, by my mother or my father, although, I can tell by the high sugar content in your blood, that you got whooped by your mamma. Indeed, my only violence at the hands of an adult was when my Daddy wouldn't wait for my mother to give birth, resulting in this twitch in my poked eye. I repaid him the favor before I could walk, or even crawl, by punching him in the eye as recompense. Ever since that point he forbade my mother to whoop me, and engaged in debate with me rather than laying on his hand, knowing that when I reached manhood, there would be pain to pay for any cruelty. But, I tell you, the fact that I knew my Daddy considered whooping me, and the fact that he kicked me out on the road as soon as I grew hair on my balls and had a chance of getting the upper hand in an altercation, set me on the road to enlightenment."

Stefan: [raises eyebrows in a penetrating, startled manner] "Okay, two out of three ain't bad. Let's go on to your specialty, understanding Black People, and see if we can shine the light of reason on many of the misconceptions held about blacks, by whites. For the sad byproduct of the recent rioting and glaring level of violence and criminality among Black Americans, is that it has reinforced and even resurrected some prejudices held by whites. So, let us, if you will, dispel some of these misconceptions that whites hold about blacks.

Mister Slickens: "Shoot, Son."

Viewer Questions

Stefan: "Okay, Mister Slickens, in preparing for your appearance on our show, my assistants worked diligently poling a random sampling of our viewership. The following are a number of questions which—if you are game—I'd like to put to you on behalf of our viewership. I would first like to point out that these are viewer questions. In fact, I will give the first names of the viewers, just so that there is no misunderstanding, as—in my estimation—some of these questions betray a certain unfortunate bias toward blacks.

"Are you ready, Mister Slickens?"

Mister Slickens: 'Shoot, son."

Stefan: "The following questions are from Steevo.

"Do all black people know how to ride wheelies right out of the womb?'

Mister Slickens: "No, only urban hoodrats are born with this natural ability, which stems from their mamma bending over for long periods while pregnant with their unfortunate asses."

Stefan: "Why do they spend three hundred dollars or more on shoes, wear them out and then get upset when something happens to them?"

Mister Slickens: "The hoodrat is born and bred to break the law and to flee the blue tentacles of the Leviathan through the crowded urban environment. Add to this the fact that the ghetto bitch that bore him is basically a reptile, who drops that bitch egg any old where and lets it hatch, while she collects the welfare and eats high on the hog. So of course, that young hopper—as we call them—needs to be fleet of foot."

Stefan: "Why do the really dark ones get black on black tattoos?"

Mister Slickens: "Because white girls get tattoos, and whatever a white girl has—like long hair—a ghetto girl must have."

Stefan: "Why do they put rims on the shittiest car or spend more on the rims then the car?"

Mister Slickens: "That is the kind of dumb shit you get when a woman raises a boy on her own. He becomes taken with shinny things and pretty stuff to a female degree."

Stefan: "The following questions were submitted by Joann. Why are black people so loud?"

Mister Slickens: "One might as well ask why white people are so inappropriately quiet. Have you ever tried listening to a heavy metal concert? Why you can't never hear that sissy white boy singing above that screaming guitar. You need to get yourself some Patty Labell of Jennifer Hudson up there so she can be heard."

Stefan: "Mister Slickens, I must interject, and point out that the best band in rock and roll history—and I don't know if you are familiar with them—was Queen. The lead vocalist, Freddie Mercury, had no such problem having his operatic quality voice being heard over the guitar."

Mister Slickens: "That is because that faggot took dick in the ass, which brought out the bitch in him."

Stefan: [Groan, accompanied by a smacking of his forehead and a pinched face grimace.] "I'm sorry for the interruption, Mister Slickens. By all means continue with your brilliant illumination of the facts!"

Mister Slickens: "As to the reason why blacks are loud and whites are quiet we need only check in with old Uncle Darwin.'

Stefan: [Groans and looks at the ceiling, working his jaw in consternation.]

Mister Slickens: "The fact of the matter is black people evolved in Africa to be noisy. After developing a taste for meat over nuts they swung down out of the trees and became the targets of lion and hyena aggression. With eat-you-alive stuff like that going down you need some noisy folks to warn the others. It's that simple.

"Similarly, with white people, we must understand that they got that way from living in caves. Just like their skin turned pale from living out of the sun and their eyes got all blued from those mammoth bone fires" [Stefan grinds the heel of his hand into his forehead and grinds his jaw.], "they evolved—devolved, actually—to be quiet, lest some dummy take up a shout and bring the entire cave down on the lot of them."

Stefan: "Why are their fewer black serial killers?

Mister Slickens: "That is an issue of classification. If all of the drug gang hitters that killed three or more niggas was classified as serial killers you'd be asking the opposite question."

Stefan: "Why do blacks hate Mexicans so much?"

Mister Slickens: "It's either that or hate their White Daddy, and that ain't happenin!"

Stefan: "The following questions are from Lisa. Why do some ghetto gibbons walk around with their hands in their pants or wear their pants so far off their asses they have to walk like a cowboy to keep them from falling down completely?"

Mister Slickens: "When a man goes to prison his belt and shoe laces are taken from him. So, when young hoppers back in the early eighties wanted to be thought of as man they'd dress like they had just been released. Although I could do without looking at that designer underwear—brought into being by this very fashion trend—I have no problem with it. It makes them slower and easier to catch when they raid my janitorial closet."

Stefan: "Why do ghetto women insult people within their hearing distance?"

Mister Slickens: "Because they are rude, stupid, and rewarded for being such, by their benevolent White Daddy, who used to be the slave master up in the big house, but is now the government."

Stefan: "Why don't they get the concept of an education or its value?"

Mister Slickens: "The education available to them has no value. Be thankful these nasty people did not pay attention in school, then they'd be hacking your bank account rather than the chain on your son's bike."

Stefan: "Why do they seem to be lacking a value system outside of materialism?"

Mister Slickens: "This goes back to slavery, in which it was made clear to these people's ancestors that a child is nothing but a good to be owned. I see whites—these days—being as prone to this bias as blacks."

Stefan: "Why do they graffitti stuff, litter so much and are so destructive?"

Miser Slickens: "These are ways to poke Whitey in the eye, small passive aggressions targeting society as a whole, which they see as their enemy."

Stefan: "Why are they always in ridiculously large groups compared to any other ethnic group?"

Mister Slickens: "Again, this goes back to slavery where blacks were predominantly worked in gangs."

Stefan: "Why do people try to talk like them when they're sub-literate sounding anyway? Or dance like them, fucking the air? Why are we emulating anything they do???"

Mister Slickens: "Obviously, because we have some pretty darned stupid white people out there!"

Stefan: "I'm hating diversity with its assumption that I'm supposed to be understanding of antisocial behaviors. It's brought me nothing but noise, violence, rudeness—crap that decreases my quality of life and endangers it. My neighborhood sucks now. I wouldn't have moved into it if it had looked like this when I was looking to buy."

Mister Slickens: "Although mankind's natural state is to dwell in ethnic communities, the government has purposefully sought to destroy community cohesion by placing the most neglected and abused segment of the population—being blacks—smack in the middle of white areas via subsidized housing and mass transit initiatives. This has the added benefit—to the government—of getting all of those stupid white people who vote to authorize increased police spending and prison construction—a boon to the Welfare State."

Stefan: "The following questions are directed to you from Ajay, who claims to be a black woman who is—this very week—leaving Baltimore due to the rampant crime and rudeness. For this we are truly sorry, Miss, and trust that your future in whatever statist paradise you have moved to is much the better."

Mister Slickens: "Baby, I'm sorry to hear you're leaving. We got few enough good sisters to be able to afford losing one. On the other hand, if you had contacted T. Spoone Slickens about your concerns earlier, he might have been able to provide some guidance and protection."

Stefan: [Rolls eyes in head before reading.] "Mister Slickens, we are running up against the clock and this lady has sent 20 questions. Perhaps we might make a speed quiz of it, a game if you will, to test your steel trap wits where all things ghetto are concerned?"

T.S.: "Bring it, Sugar Britches!"

Stefan: "Why do they have big lips and little ears?"

T.S.: "From going down on the white masters who bred us as they bastard slaves—hence the adoration of Angelina Jolee."

Stefan: "Why do they have big butts?"

T.S.: "Oh, you a no-booty sista for sure. To hold Master's weak-ass up while they getting busy up in the big house, which is apt to be in a hurry so that Mistress don't catch his ass in the act."

Stefan: "Why do they have thick tongues?"

T.S.: "That is another epironogonetic " [Stefan groans] response to oppression, so the negro tongue did not get poisoned from all of that shoe polish—which is almost always got to be black or brown don't you know, puttin' the metaphor right into that boot lickin' mouth!"

Stefan: "Why are they so loud?

T.S.: "Lions and hyenas—next question."

Stefan: "Why do they dress like gangsters and ho's?"

T.S.: "Because they are—girl, get your behind to the country and close the door. It's a miracle you survived up in here."

Stefan: "Why do they like to bring attention to themselves?"

T.S.: "It's a deception, tried and true, so you don't see they greedy hand in your pocket taking your last dollar!"

Stefan: "Why are they so lazy?"

T.S.: "Because that lazy white muvasuca up on the porch of that big house fathered them bastards, and the apple don't fall far from the tree."

Stefan: "Why are they always complaining?"

T.S.: "Because they are raised by bitches, and what does a bitch do but bitch about every old thing?"

Stefan: "Why are they always bringing up the past—bringing up slavery—instead of living for now?"

T.S.: "Because the slave's lot in life was so sorrowful and the 'now' sucked so bad he got to reminiscing about the past—even if he didn't know jack about it."

Stefan: "Why is their first reaction to a problem to be violent?"

T.S.: "Girl, you bring up a race of folks at the whipping post, what you think you gonna git but whooping?"

Stefan: "Why are they always making up words? What's wrong with the words that have already been created in the dictionary?"

T.S.: "It's easier then remembering the real words."

Stefan: "Why do they tease or put down other black people that speak and dress well?"

T.S.: "Because you're too good for them niggas, girl, and they know it—and are trying to keep you from realizing it."

Stefan: "Why are the ones that drive nice cars have crappy apartments?"

T.S.: "A vacant stash house is a dime a dozen, but a good getaway car is hard to come by."

Stefan: "Why are so many on public assistance?"

T.S.: "Because they was bred to be a dependent race. The independent thinkers who tried to strike out on their own were killed off.

Stefan: "Why do they have so many children that they can't take care of?"

T.S.: "White Daddy has that covered with his welfare bullshit."

Stefan: "Why are they always trying to scam people?"

T.S.: "Because they take after their White Daddy, who is the government, and what does a government do but scam folks?"

Stefan: "Why do they get tattoos? You can't see them most of the time because their skin is too dark."

T.S.: "Because they're dumbasses."

Stefan: "Why can't they throw their fake hair out in the trash can? When you see the hair blowing across the road it looks scary."

T.S.: "What a unicorn you are. They don't throw that shit out. Some other bitch ripped it off they head while they was rumbling in the asphalt jungle."

Stefan: "Why do they smell like the food they cook?"

T.S.: "Because they cook with heavy grease, a legacy of coming up on a pork-fed plantation, and the grease makes the scent stick to their clothes."

Stefan: "Why are they always spitting, both men and women?"

T.S.: "Because, deep down, they know themselves to still be slaves, slaves to the government that made those sidewalks, and that is their little bit of unconscious rebellion— all they can manage on a day to day, short of going into crime.

Stefan: "Mister Slickens, it has been a pleasure to have you on the show, and, although this was probably a onetime occurrence, I have –well, I've had my eyes opened. Thank you for joining us today."

Mister Slickens: "Your welcome, and thank you, Steven Molay for helping me say my piece."

[Stefan grabs his ears and grimaces at the ceiling and the video cuts away…]

There is no truth to the rumors that Mister Slickens will be meeting Justin W. R. Justice in a debate.

www.ingramcontent.com/pod-product-compliance
Lightning Source LLC
Chambersburg PA
CBHW071346280526
45787CB00001B/235